BEReF

# Tolley's Income Tax 2004 Post-Budget Supplement

by
David Smailes FCA

LexisNexis™ UK

**Members of the LexisNexis Group worldwide**

| | |
|---|---|
| United Kingdom | LexisNexis UK, a Division of Reed Elsevier (UK) Ltd, Halsbury House, 35 Chancery Lane, LONDON, WC2A 1EL, and 4 Hill Street, EDINBURGH EH2 3JZ |
| Argentina | LexisNexis Argentina, BUENOS AIRES |
| Australia | LexisNexis Butterworths, CHATSWOOD, New South Wales |
| Austria | LexisNexis Verlag ARD Orac GmbH & Co KG, VIENNA |
| Canada | LexisNexis Butterworths, MARKHAM, Ontario |
| Chile | LexisNexis Chile Ltda, SANTIAGO DE CHILE |
| Czech Republic | Nakladatelství Orac sro, PRAGUE |
| France | Editions du Juris-Classeur SA, PARIS |
| Germany | LexisNexis Deutschland GmbH, FRANKFURT, MUNSTER |
| Hong Kong | LexisNexis Butterworths, HONG KONG |
| Hungary | HVG-Orac, BUDAPEST |
| India | LexisNexis Butterworths, NEW DELHI |
| Ireland | LexisNexis, DUBLIN |
| Italy | Giuffrè Editore, MILAN |
| Malaysia | Malayan Law Journal Sdn Bhd, KUALA LUMPUR |
| New Zealand | LexisNexis Butterworths, WELLINGTON |
| Poland | Wydawnictwo Prawnicze LexisNexis, WARSAW |
| Singapore | LexisNexis Butterworths, SINGAPORE |
| South Africa | LexisNexis Butterworths, DURBAN |
| Switzerland | Stämpfli Verlag AG, BERNE |
| USA | LexisNexis, DAYTON, Ohio |

© Reed Elsevier (UK) Ltd 2004

Published by LexisNexis UK

Crown copyright material is reproduced with the permission of the Controller of HMSO and the Queen's Printer for Scotland. Any European material in this work which has been reproduced from EUR-lex, the official European Communities legislation website, is European Communities copyright.

A CIP Catalogue record for this book is available from the British Library.

ISBN  0 7545 2545 7

Printed and bound in Great Britain by Hobbs the Printers Ltd, Totton, Hampshire

Visit LexisNexis UK at www.lexisnexis.co.uk

# About This Supplement

This Supplement to Tolley's Income Tax 2003/04 gives details of changes in the law and practice of UK income tax from 2 July 2003 to 17 March 2004 (immediately before the Chancellor's Budget speech on that day). It lists the changes in the same order and under the same paragraph headings as the annual publication. Also included is a summary of the Chancellor's Budget proposals.

Each time Tolley's Income Tax 2003/04 is used, reference should be made to the material contained in this Supplement. The *Contents* give a list of all the chapters and paragraphs which have been updated.

TOLLEY

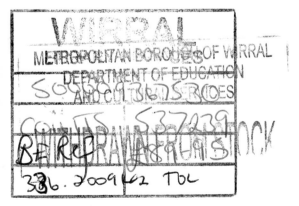

# Contents

This Supplement contains amendments to the chapters and paragraphs of Tolley's Income Tax 2003/04 as listed below.

# Contents

# Contents

# Contents

**Budget Summary 2004**

# 1  Allowances and Tax Rates

1.14  **Personal allowance.** The personal allowance for 2004/05 is £4,745 (*SI 2003 No 3215*). The second table on page 11 is updated to include 2004/05 figures as follows (see Pre-Budget Report, December 2003).

|  |  | Personal allowance | | Income | Maximum income | |
|---|---|---|---|---|---|---|
|  |  | 65 to 74 | 75 or over | limit | 65 to 74 | 75 or over |
| For | 2004/05 | £6,830 | £6,950 | £18,900 | £23,070 | £23,310 |

1.15  **Married couple's allowance.** The paragraph spanning pages 12 and 13 is replaced with the following.

'*Spouse reaching age 65 before 6 April 2000.* As indicated above, following the general abolition of the married couple's allowance for 2000/01 and subsequent years of assessment, it continues to be available at the 10% rate where either spouse was born before 6 April 1935. In such cases (and also for years prior to 2000/01), where the claimant or his wife is at any time in the year of assessment aged 65 (or aged 75) or over, or would have been but for his or her death in that year, a higher allowance is available (but with relief restricted, and calculated, as above). Where the claimant's total income exceeds an income limit (as in 1.14 above), that higher allowance is reduced by one half of the excess (less any reduction made in the claimant's personal allowance age increase, see 1.14 above) until the allowance is the same as the ordinary married couple's allowance. As a consequence of the abolition of the ordinary married couple's allowance for 2000/01 and subsequent years of assessment, the minimum figure is based on the ordinary 1999/2000 figure above, indexed for future years in the normal way (see 1.13 above).

| For | 2000/01 | £2,000 |
|---|---|---|
| For | 2001/02 | £2,070 |
| For | 2002/03 | £2,110 |
| For | 2003/04 | £2,150 |
| For | 2004/05 | £2,210* |

\* see *SI 2003 No 3215*

The maximum income level at which the higher allowance ceases is shown in the right hand column below.'

The first table on page 13 is updated to include 2004/05 figures as follows (see *SI 2003 No 3215*).

|  |  | Married couple's allowance | | Income | Maximum income | |
|---|---|---|---|---|---|---|
|  |  | 65 to 74 | 75 or over | limit | 65 to 74 | 75 or over |
| For | 2004/05 | £5,725 | £5,795 | £18,900 | £30,100 | £30,480 |

1.19  **Blind persons.** The blind person's allowance for 2004/05 is £1,560 (*SI 2003 No 3215*).

# 3  Anti-Avoidance

3.2  **Cancellation of tax advantages from certain transactions in securities.** The opening paragraph is replaced with the following.

# 3    Anti-Avoidance

'Where, in consequence of transaction(s) in securities (including interests in companies not limited by shares, and such transaction(s) coupled with liquidation of a company), *combined with* any of the relevant circumstances mentioned below, a person is able to obtain a tax advantage, the Board of Inland Revenue may make adjustments counteracting that advantage (having first given notice of their intention to do so), unless the person concerned is able to show that the transactions were made (1) for *bona fide* commercial reasons or in the ordinary course of investment management, and (2) without tax advantages being their main object, or one of their main objects. [*ICTA 1988, s 703*]. For 'transactions in securities' see *CIR v Joiner HL 1975, 50 TC 449* (in which a variation of rights prior to a liquidation was held to be such a transaction) and *CIR v Laird Group plc HL, [2003] STC 1349* (in which the payment of a dividend representing previously undistributed profits was held not to be). For '*bona fide* commercial reasons' see *Laird Group* in the *Ch D ([2001] STC 689)* and *CIR v Brebner HL 1967, 43 TC 705, Clark v CIR Ch D 1978, 52 TC 482* and *Marwood Homes Ltd v CIR, Tribunal 1998, [1999] SSCD 44*. In *Lewis (as a trustee of the Redrow Staff Pension Scheme) v CIR (Sp C 218), [1999] SSCD 349*, a distribution by way of purchase of its own shares by a company from the trustees of its pension scheme, pursuant to legislation requiring the trustees to reduce their holding, was held to be a transaction carried out by the trustees both for *bona fide* commercial reasons and in the ordinary course of investment management.'

The last two sentences of the first paragraph on page 27 are replaced with the following.

'On the question of whether a tax advantage was a 'main object' of a transaction, see *Marwood Homes Ltd v CIR, Tribunal 1998, [1999] SSCD 44*. See also *Laird Group plc v CIR Ch D, [2001] STC 689*.'

In the penultimate paragraph (page 28), the name of Margaret Draper is substituted for that of Ray McCann.

3.5 **Treatment of price differential on sale and repurchase of securities.** At the end (page 32), the following is added.

'For a brief overview of the changes made by *FA 2003* to the tax provisions on sale and repurchase agreements, see Revenue Tax Bulletin August 2003 pp 1052, 1053.'

3.7 **'Manufactured' dividends or interest.** At the end of the second paragraph, the following is added.

'Where, after 5 November 2003, an individual receives a real or manufactured dividend in respect of UK shares acquired under a repo or stock lending arrangement on terms requiring him to manufacture an equivalent payment, legislation in *FA 2004* will seek to ensure that the manufactured payment is deductible only from the dividend receipt and not from total income as normal; in addition, no tax is treated as having been paid at source on the dividend received (Revenue Press Release 6 November 2003).' See also the Budget Summary.

The paragraph on page 35 beginning 'As regards (*c*) above ...' is replaced with the following.

'As regards (*c*) above, the Board was able before 1 November 2003 to arrange for manufactured overseas dividends to be paid without deduction of tax in certain cases where a double taxation agreement is in force with the territory in which the recipient of the dividend (not being UK resident) is resident. See *SI 1993 No 1957* as amended by *SI 1995 No 1551* and *SI 1996 No 2654* and revoked by *SI 2003 No 2581*. From 1 November 2003, the general requirement for the payer to deduct and account for tax in relation to payments of manufactured overseas dividends to non-UK recipients is removed by *SI 2003 No 2582*.'

3.9 **Transfer pricing.** At the end of the paragraph beginning 'For 1999/2000 and subsequent years of assessment', the following is added.

'It was announced in the December 2003 Pre-Budget Report that *Schedule 28AA* is to be extended from 1 April 2004 to transactions both parties to which are in the UK, but there will be exemptions for small and medium-sized businesses; details and draft legislation are on the Revenue website.' See also the Budget Summary.

3.24    **Arrangements for continued free use of assets once owned ('pre-owned assets').** At the end of chapter, the following new paragraph 3.24 is added.

'It was announced in the December 2003 Pre-Budget Report that an income tax charge under Schedule D, Case VI is to be imposed from 2005/06 onwards on the annual benefit of using an asset that was once owned by the user, and has not been sold to an unconnected party at arm's length, where such use is enjoyed free of charge or at below market rent. The charge will also apply to replacement assets and to assets which the user did not formerly own but which are purchased with funds provided by him. The legislation will be in *FA 2004* and will include rules for valuing the benefit — probably market rent for real property and a percentage of capital value (possibly using the 'official rate' at 75.20 SCHEDULE E — EMPLOYMENT INCOME) for other property. A set-off will be allowed for any actual rent paid for the benefit. There will be a substantial *de minimis* exclusion (the amount of which remains undecided), and incidental use will also be disregarded. If the donor has expressly reserved a right to continuing use of a gifted asset, presumably such that the Gifts with Reservation rules apply — see Tolley's Inheritance Tax, the asset will not fall within this income tax charge. Pre-existing arrangements will escape the new charge if they are dismantled, or the user begins paying full market rent, before the start date of 6 April 2005.' See also the Budget Summary.

# 4    Appeals

4.2    **Time limit for appeals etc.** At the end, the following is added.

'*TMA 1970, s 49* confers upon the Commissioners a broader discretion than that of the inspector; they should take interests of justice into account; lack of reasonable excuse is potentially relevant but not conclusive (*R (oao Browallia Cal Ltd) v City of London Commrs QB, 2003 STI 2220*).'

4.17    **Hearing and determination of proceedings.** At the end of the first paragraph, the following is added.

'See *Businessman v Inspector of Taxes (Sp C 374), [2003] SSCD 403* for a direction that the whole hearing be in private for the protection of the taxpayer's private life.'

In the penultimate paragraph (page 75), the following is added to the list of cases in which the taxpayer's application for costs was refused: *Lavery v Macleod (No 2) (Sp C 375), [2003] SSCD 413*.

4.24    **Judicial review.** At the top of page 81, the following is added.

'A further application for judicial review on the grounds that the Revenue's refusal to repay was unfair was similarly dismissed (*R (oao Carvill) v CIR (No 2) QB, [2003] STC 1539*).'

# 5    Assessments

5.3    **Further assessments on 'discovery'.** The fourth paragraph from the end (on page 86) is replaced with the following.

'The categories in (i)–(iv) above constitute an exhaustive definition of 'information made available to an officer of the Board' for the purpose of (2)(*b*) above; an officer is not precluded from making a discovery assessment simply because some other information (not normally part of the officer's immediate checks) might be available (in the instant case a form P11D) that might place doubt on the sufficiency of the self-assessment (*Veltema v Langham CA, 2004 STI 501*).'

# 6    Back Duty

6.11    **Offers by taxpayer.** At the end of the first paragraph on page 99, the following is added.

'In *R v Gill and another CA, [2003] STC 1229*, the facts in which pre-dated the November 2002 revision, it was held that Code C of *Police and Criminal Evidence Act 1984* applied to the 'Hansard' interview (in which, in the instant case, the taxpayers made statements later used by the Revenue in a successful criminal prosecution) and the taxpayers should, accordingly, have been cautioned and the interview taped. The Revenue have since adopted this approach; the taxpayer or his adviser should be provided with a copy of the tape.'

# 10    Capital Allowances

10.5    **Cemeteries and crematoria.** In the second paragraph on page 125, the reference to the Revenue Inspector's Manual is replaced by a reference to Revenue Business Income Manual BIM 52505, 52510. In the fourth paragraph on that page, the reference to the Revenue Inspector's Manual is replaced by a reference to Revenue Business Income Manual BIM 52520, 52525.

10.25    **Eligible expenditure.** At the foot of page 159, the following is added to the list of items held *not* to be plant: 'an all-weather horse racing track (*Shove v Lingfield Park 1991 Ltd Ch D, [2003] STC 1003*)'.

10.27    **First-year allowances.** In sub-paragraph (v) on pages 167, 168 (exclusion of leased plant and machinery), the following is added.

'Expenditure by a company on plant and machinery to be used by its subsidiary in return for an annual charge fell within the exclusion (*M F Freeman (Plant) Ltd v Jowett (Sp C 376), [2003] SSCD 423*).'

In the definition of '*small or medium-sized enterprise*' (page 169), it is noted that the first two of the three quoted thresholds are increased to £22.8 million and £11.4 million respectively for accounting periods ending on or after 30 January 2004. There is provision to prevent the benefit of the increased limits being brought forward by a change of accounting date. See Revenue Press Release 30 January 2004 and *SI 2004 No 16*.

In the definition of '*small enterprise*' immediately following, it is noted that the first two of the three quoted thresholds are doubled for accounting periods ending on or after 30 January 2004. There is provision to prevent the benefit of the increased limits being brought forward by a change of accounting date. See Revenue Press Release 30 January 2004 and *SI 2004 No 16*.

The definition of 'energy-saving plant or machinery' is rewritten as follows (see *SI 2003 No 1744*).

"*Energy-saving plant or machinery*', for the purposes of (*d*) above, is plant or machinery which, either at the time the expenditure is incurred or at the time the contract for its provision

4

is entered into, is of a description specified by Treasury order *and* meets the energy-saving criteria specified by Treasury order for plant or machinery of that description. Expenditure incurred, or incurred under a contract entered into, after 31 March 2001 but before 16 July 2001 (the date of making of the first Treasury order) qualifies if it would have done so had that order already been made when the expenditure was incurred. A Treasury order may identify qualifying plant or machinery by reference to lists of technology or products issued by the relevant Secretary of State; the first order refers to the Energy Technology Product List (ETPL) initially published on 1 April 2001 (and available at www.eca.gov.uk). An order may also provide that, in specified cases, no FYA is to be given under (*d*) above unless a '*relevant certificate of energy efficiency*' is in force, i.e. a certificate issued by the Secretary of State, the Scottish Ministers, the Welsh Assembly or the relevant NI department, or by persons authorised by them, to the effect that a particular item, or an item constructed to a particular design, meets the relevant energy-saving criteria. The first order so specifies certain combined heat and power equipment. With effect after 4 August 2003, component based fixed systems falling within the technology class 'automatic monitoring and targeting equipment' (see below) were also specified. If a certificate is revoked, it is treated as having never been in issue, with the result that FYAs under (*d*) above will not have been available. Subject to penalty under *TMA 1970, s 98* for non-compliance, a person who has consequently made an incorrect tax return must give notice to the Revenue, specifying the amendment required to the return, within three months of his becoming aware of the problem. Technology classes initially included in the ETPL, subject to the appropriate criteria, certification or product approval, were boilers, combined heat and power, lighting, motors and drives, pipework insulation, refrigeration and thermal screens. The following were added with effect after 4 August 2002: heat pumps for space heating, radiant and warm air heaters, compressed air equipment and solar thermal systems. With effect after 4 August 2003, automatic monitoring and targeting equipment was added. If one or more components of an item of plant and machinery qualify under these provisions, but the whole item does not, normal apportionment rules are disapplied, and instead the first-year qualifying expenditure under (*d*) above is limited to the amount (or aggregate amount) specified in the ETPL for that component (or those components); where relevant, each *instalment* of expenditure falls to be apportioned in the same way as the whole. See generally the detailed Guidance Notes published on the Revenue website on 13 March 2002.'

The definition of 'environmentally beneficial plant or machinery' (page 170) is rewritten as follows (see *SI 2003 No 2076*).

"*Environmentally beneficial plant or machinery*', for the purposes of (*h*) above, is plant or machinery which, either at the time the expenditure is incurred or at the time the contract for its provision is entered into, is of a description specified by Treasury order *and* meets the environmental criteria specified by Treasury order for plant or machinery of that description. A Treasury order may identify qualifying plant or machinery by reference to technology lists or product lists issued by the relevant Secretary of State. The intention is to promote the use of technologies, or products, designed to remedy or prevent damage to the physical environment or natural resources (Revenue Press Release BN 26, 9 April 2003); the first order refers to the Water Technology Product List (WTPL) initially published in April 2003 (and available at www.eca-water.gov.uk). Expenditure incurred, or incurred under a contract entered into, after 31 March 2003 but before 11 August 2003 (the date of making of the first Treasury order) qualifies if it would have done so had that order already been made when the expenditure was incurred or the contract entered into. An order may provide that, in specified cases, no FYA is to be given under (*h*) above unless a '*relevant certificate of environmental benefit*' is in force, i.e. a certificate issued by the Secretary of State, the Scottish Ministers, the Welsh Assembly or the relevant NI department, or by persons authorised by them, to the effect that a particular item, or an item constructed to a particular design, meets the relevant environmental criteria (though the first order makes no such provision). If a certificate is revoked, it is treated as having never been in issue, with the result that FYAs under (*h*) above will not have been available. Subject to penalty under *TMA 1970, s 98* for non-compliance, a person who has consequently made an incorrect tax return must give notice to the Revenue, specifying the amendment required to the return, within three months of his becoming aware of the problem. Technology classes initially included in the WTPL, subject to the appropriate criteria or product approval, are water meters, flow controllers, leakage detection equipment, low flush toilets and efficient taps. If one or more components of an item of plant and machinery qualify under these provisions, but the whole item does not, normal apportionment rules are disapplied, and instead the first-year qualifying expenditure under (*h*) above is limited to the amount (or aggregate amount) specified in the WTPL for that component (or those components); where relevant, each *instalment* of expenditure falls to be apportioned in the same way as the whole.'

10.38   **Plant and machinery — miscellaneous.** In sub-paragraph (H), the last sentence of the second paragraph is replaced with the following.

'For further details of 'renewals basis' and change from renewals basis to normal capital allowances and *vice versa*, see Revenue Pamphlet IR 1, B1 as revised and Revenue Business Income Manual BIM 46935, 46950, 46955.'

A new third paragraph is then added as follows.

'A **valuation basis** is a variation of renewals basis in which a class of assets, for example spare parts for plant and machinery, are dealt with in a similar way to trading stock, involving opening and closing valuations. For further detail, and for change from capital allowances to valuation basis, see Revenue Business Income Manual BIM 46940, 46960.'

10.52   **Research and development (formerly scientific research).** The last full paragraph on page 237 is replaced with the following (and see also 71.80 below).

''*Research and development*' is as defined by *ICTA 1988, s 837A* and supporting regulations (see 71.80 SCHEDULE D, CASES I AND II), but also includes oil and gas exploration and appraisal (within *ICTA 1988, s 837B*). [*CAA 2001, s 437(2); CAA 1990, s 139(1)*].'

# 14   Certificates of Tax Deposit

14.1   **Introduction.** This section is replaced with the following.

'Taxpayers may make deposits, evidenced by Certificates of Tax Deposit, with Collectors of Taxes for the subsequent payment of their own tax and Class 4 NIC liabilities generally (other than PAYE and tax deducted from payments to construction sub-contractors and corporation tax — see further below). If a deposit is tendered in respect of any liability, that liability will be treated as paid on the later of the certificate date and the normal due date for that liability (see 56 PAYMENT OF TAX). The minimum initial deposit is £500 with minimum additions of £250. Deposits of £100,000 or over must be made by direct remittance to the Bank of England.

Series 7 Certificates are *not* available for purchase for use against corporation tax liabilities.

Deposits made after 5 April 2003 in a partnership name are not accepted in settlement of an individual partner's tax liability.

Interest, which is payable gross but taxable, will accrue for a maximum of six years from the date of deposit to the date of payment of tax or, if earlier, the 'deemed due date' for payment of the liability against which the deposit (plus accrued interest) is set. The '*deemed due date*' is generally the normal due date for payment of the tax under the relevant legislation, and does not change if for any reason an assessment is made late or the liability is not payable until later (e.g. following settlement of an appeal). A deposit may be withdrawn for cash at any time but will then receive a reduced rate of interest. Where a certificate is used in settlement of a tax liability, interest at the higher rate up to the normal due date may be less than interest at the encashment rate up to the reckonable date. In such circumstances the taxpayer may instruct the Revenue to calculate interest on the latter basis. (ICAEW Technical Release TAX 13/93, 30 June 1993). The rates of interest, published by the Treasury, and calculated by reference to the rate on comparable investment with the Government, vary with the size and period of the deposit, and the rate payable on a deposit is adjusted to the current rate on each anniversary of the deposit.

Deposits are not transferable except to personal representatives of a deceased person.

Rates of interest are given at 14.2, 14.3 and 14.4 below. Information on current rates may be obtained from www.inlandrevenue.gov.uk/howtopay/ctd_interest_rates.pdf, from any Revenue Tax Collecting Office or from Revenue Finance at 01903 509064 or 509066 or 01903 700222 ext. 2064/2066.'

14.2    The following entries are added to the list of rates for deposits of less than £100,000.

|  | Used to pay tax | Withdrawals for cash |
|---|---|---|
| 11 July 2003–6 November 2003 | nil | nil |
| 7 November 2003–5 February 2004 | ¼% | nil |
| 6 February 2004 onwards | ½% | ¼% |

14.3    The following entries are added to the list of rates for deposits of £100,000 or more used to meet a scheduled liability.

|  |  | Period of deposit in months | | | |
|---|---|---|---|---|---|
|  | Under 1 | 1 but under 3 | 3 but under 6 | 6 but under 9 | 9 but under 12 |
| 11 July 2003–6 November 2003 | nil | 2½% | 2¼% | 2% | 2% |
| 7 November 2003–5 February 2004 | ¼% | 3% | 3% | 3% | 3% |
| 6 February 2004 onwards | ½% | 3% | 3% | 3% | 3% |

14.4    The following entries are added to the list of rates for deposits of £100,000 or more withdrawn for cash.

|  |  | Period of deposit in months | | | |
|---|---|---|---|---|---|
|  | Under 1 | 1 but under 3 | 3 but under 6 | 6 but under 9 | 9 but under 12 |
| 11 July 2003–6 November 2003 | Nil | 1¼% | 1% | 1% | 1% |
| 7 November 2003–5 February 2004 | Nil | 1½% | 1½% | 1½% | 1½% |
| 6 February 2004 onwards | ¼% | 1½% | 1½% | 1½% | 1½% |

# 15   Charities

15.10   **Restrictions on exemptions.** Immediately before the paragraph beginning 'Qualifying loans' on page 260, the following paragraph is added.

'There is guidance at www.inlandrevenue.gov.uk/charities/annex_iii.htm as to the approach the Revenue adopt in deciding whether or not a particular investment is a qualifying investment. As regards swap contracts, e.g. interest rate or currency swaps, see Revenue Tax Bulletin August 2003 p 1056.'

15.18   **Payroll giving schemes.** In the penultimate paragraph, passing reference is made to *SI 2003 No 1745*.

## 17    Claims

17.5    **General.** The final paragraph is replaced with the following two paragraphs.

*'Telephone claims and other services.* The Board have powers to accept income tax claims by telephone (or by any other method not in writing), where a written claim would otherwise be required, for which purpose they must publish general directions as regards the circumstances in which, and conditions subject to which, such claims will be accepted. The time for making the claim and the contents may not be altered by the directions. No directions may be given in relation to claims by an individual as trustee, partner or personal representative, to CAPITAL ALLOWANCES (10) claims or to claims under *TMA 1970, Sch 1B* (see 17.2 above). Directions may similarly be given as regards the making of elections, the giving of notice, the amendment or withdrawal of claims, elections and notices and the amendment of returns. [*FA 1998, s 118*].

All tax offices now offer certain telephone services, as set out in Revenue Pamphlet IR 131, SP 2/03 (replacing SP 2/98) and, for tax offices served by a Call Centre, Revenue Pamphlet IR 131, SP 3/03 (replacing SP 8/98) with which are published the appropriate directions. These include acceptance of telephone claims for personal allowances, interest relief and most employment expenses. They also enable taxpayers to notify changes in their details, including changes to employment benefits-in-kind. Call Centres will additionally accept telephone amendments to self-assessment tax returns. These services are available to individuals and, subject to identity and authorisation checks, to agents acting for individuals.'

## 21    Construction Industry Tax Scheme

21.1    **Scheme applicable from 1 August 1999.** At the beginning, the following new paragraph is added.

'**Proposed future changes.** It was announced in the December 2003 Pre-Budget Report that a new Construction Industry Tax Scheme is to be introduced from April 2006, with the legislation to be included in *FA 2004*; in the meantime, the Revenue are increasing compliance activities in the sector.'

21.4    **Sub-contractors' tax certificates.** The penultimate paragraph (page 313) is slightly rewritten as follows.

'*Changes in a business.* Where an individual or firm incorporates, or a partnership becomes a sole trader, the new business will require a new certificate. However, if the business is essentially the same, the new business may apply immediately on the basis of turnover of the old business, using either the three-year test (at 21.5 below), applied in the light of the particular circumstances of the case, or the six-month test (also at 21.5 below), depending on how long the old business existed. Changes in the number of partners in a firm or directors/shareholders in a company, without any change in the business, do not require the turnover test to be re-applied before the certificate falls to be renewed, unless the inspector suspects manipulation of the threshold provisions. New partners/directors can apply for additional certificates. (Revenue Pamphlet IR 40(CIS) pp 6, 7).'

21.5    **Turnover test.** The first paragraph is slightly rewritten as follows.

'*Individuals (other than in relation to applications as partners in firms).* The turnover test requires the applicant to satisfy the Board that, during the period of validity of the certificate, the aggregate annual amount of 'relevant payments' received is likely to be not less than the 'individual turnover threshold' of £30,000. (It should, however, be noted that Revenue Pamphlet IR 40(CIS) states (at Appendix 1): 'If you are using the six-month test, you should show the actual amount you *received* in the period. Where you are using a three-year test on the basis of accounts, we would not expect you to adjust figures for gross construction turnover and materials for debtors or creditors to arrive at the net "payments received" in the three years. Just use the figures earned for construction operations, as shown in your accounts.'.) '*Relevant payments*' are all payments, net of the cost of materials, under contracts relating to, or to the work of individuals participating in the carrying out of, construction operations (see 21.2 above), whether or not within the scheme (i.e. including work for private householders, etc.).'

# 22   Deceased Estates

22.2    **Liability of personal representatives.** At the end, the following paragraph is added.

'Strictly, the personal representatives should notify the Revenue that they are liable to tax on estate income no later than six months after the tax year in which they become liable (in accordance with 57.1 PENALTIES) and should file self-assessment tax returns and pay any tax due on normal self-assessment payment dates (see 78.4–78.7 SELF-ASSESSMENT). However, the Revenue operate informal procedures as follows. For estates where date of death is after 5 April 2003, they will instead accept a single computation and one-off payment of an estate's self-assessment liability (presumably including capital gains tax where relevant) if the estate is not 'complex' and the liability (over the whole of the administration period) is less than £10,000. For these purposes, an estate is '*complex*' if probate value exceeds £2.5 million *or* if administration continues into the third tax year from date of death *or* the personal representatives have disposed of a chargeable asset of the estate for more than £250,000. For estates where date of death was on or before 5 April 2003, the Revenue allowed one-off payment only where probate value was less than £400,000. (Revenue Tax Bulletin August 2003 pp 1043, 1044). The Tax Bulletin article also provides information as to which tax office is likely to deal with an estate.'

# 25   Double Tax Relief

25.2    **Double tax agreements.** New agreements with Australia (*SI 2003 No 3199*), Canada (*SI 2003 No 2619*), Chile (*SI 2003 No 3200*) and Mauritius (*SI 2003 No 2620* — protocol) are added to the list on pages 348, 349. The agreement with Australia applies from *broadly* 6 April 2004 (UK) and 1 July 2004 (Australia) — see Revenue Press Release 19 January 2004 for further detail. The Mauritius protocol applies from 6 April 2003 (UK) and 1 July 2003 (Mauritius). The others have not yet entered into force.

In the paragraph on page 347 headed 'Under many double tax agreements …', the last sentence is replaced with the following.

'In the absence of a formal contract of employment, the Revenue would not consider a UK company to be the employer of a short-term business visitor who is in the UK for less than 60 days in a tax year (the '**60-day rule**'), provided that that period does not form part of a more substantial period (for example, a period spanning two tax years) when the taxpayer is in the UK (Revenue Tax Bulletins October 1996 p 358, December 2003 pp 1069–1071).'

25.4    **Unilateral relief by UK.** In sub-paragraph (*a*) on page 351, the reference to the Revenue Inspector's Manual is replaced by a reference to Revenue Business Income Manual BIM 45905.

## 26 Enterprise Investment Scheme

25.5 **Specific matters.** Sub-paragraph (*i*) on page 354 is replaced with the following.

'**Notional Tax.** Under *ICTA 1988, s 788(5)* it may be provided that any tax which would have been payable in a foreign country but for a relief under the law of that territory given with a view to promoting industrial, commercial, scientific, educational or other development therein is nevertheless treated for purposes of credit against UK tax as if it had been paid. See, for example, Revenue Double Taxation Relief Manual at DT 12758 in the case of Malaysia and at DT 16911 in the case of Singapore. For restrictions on relief available to companies in respect of such notional tax, see Tolley's Corporation Tax under Double Tax Relief.'

## 26 Enterprise Investment Scheme

26.2 **Conditions for relief.** At the end of the paragraph spanning pages 359 and 360, the following sentence is added.

'Paragraphs (*b*) and (*c*) above are *not* satisfied if the money raised by the issue is used partly to pay dividends to investors (*Forthright (Wales) Ltd v Inspector of Taxes (Sp C 383) 2003, [2004] SSCD 35*).'

26.6 **Qualifying business activities.** At the top of page 367, the cross-reference to 10.52 CAPITAL ALLOWANCES is replaced with a cross-reference to 71.80 SCHEDULE D, CASES I AND II and it is noted that, for EIS purposes, the latest DTI guidelines issued on 5 March 2004 have no effect in relation to shares issued before 6 April 2004.

26.10 **Limits on relief.** At the end of the second full paragraph (upper limit on investment), it is noted that the December 2003 Pre-Budget Report included a proposal to increase the £150,000 limit to £200,000 from 6 April 2004.' See also the Budget Summary.

## 27 European Community Legislation

27.3 **Current Directives.** The full text is replaced with the following.

'In contrast to the extensive application of EU legislation in the VAT sphere, direct taxes are currently subject to only the following specific measures.

(*a*)    *Council Regulation 2137/85* (25 July 1985) concerning European Economic Interest Groupings.

(*b*)    *Directive 90/434/EEC* (23 July 1990) concerning mergers, divisions, transfers of assets and exchanges of shares concerning companies of different Member States.

(*c*)    *Directive 90/435/EEC* (23 July 1990) concerning distributions of profits to parent companies.

(*d*)    *Directive 2003/48/EC* (3 June 2003) concerning the taxation of savings income.

(*e*)    *Directive 2003/49/EC* (3 June 2003) concerning interest and royalty payments.

As regards (*a*), see the related UK legislation at 53.19 PARTNERSHIPS. As regards (*b*), the UK legislation is dealt with in Tolley's Corporation Tax under Capital Gains. As regards (*c*), a minor amendment is dealt with at 23.12 DEDUCTION OF TAX AT SOURCE, and see also Tolley's Corporation Tax under Double Tax Relief. As regards (*d*), see 67.16 RETURNS and as regards (*e*), see Tolley's Corporation Tax under Income Tax in relation to a Company. The Revenue

Consultative Document on EC Direct Tax Measures published in December 1991 sets out the manner in which (*b*) and (*c*) are considered to be implemented by the UK legislative changes.

For a case on the application of *Directive 90/434/EEC*, see *Leur-Bloem v Inspecteur der Belastingdienst/Ondernemingen Amsterdam 2 (Case C-28/95) ECJ, [1997] STC 1205.*

In addition to the above, *Convention 90/436/EEC* (23 July 1990), concerning arbitration in double taxation disputes arising from transfer pricing adjustments, came into force on 1 January 1995. See 3.9 ANTI-AVOIDANCE, 25.5(*m*) DOUBLE TAX RELIEF and 36.2(*o*), 36.4 INLAND REVENUE: CONFIDENTIALITY OF INFORMATION.

27.4     **Future developments.** The full text is replaced with the following.

'The European Commission has proposed to amend the Parent-Subsidiary Directive (*90/435/ EEC*) and the Mergers Directive (*90/434/EEC*). See the corresponding chapter of Tolley's Corporation Tax.

*The European Company Statute Regulation (Council Regulation (EC) No 2157/2001)*, which was adopted on 8 October 2001, will apply to all Member States with effect from 8 October 2004. It will create the legal framework for a new corporate entity, the European Company or 'Societas Europaea' (SE), to facilitate cross-border activities within the European Union including cross-border mergers. See the corresponding chapter of Tolley's Corporation Tax.'

# 29   Exempt Income

29.11    **Individual savings accounts.** After the first paragraph, the following paragraph is added.

'It was announced in the December 2003 Pre-Budget Report that the insurance component is to be abolished from April 2005. Life insurance products and newly-introduced medium-term stakeholder products will instead go into the stocks and shares component, except that products which provide a 'cash-like' return (i.e. which are relatively risk-free) will have to go into the cash component. The maximum subscription per tax year to a stocks and shares mini-account will be increased from £3,000 to £4,000.'

At the end of the paragraph on page 406 beginning 'A mini-account …', the following sentence is added.

'From April 2005, as a consequence of the abolition of the insurance component (see above), the maximum subscription to a stocks and shares mini-account is expected to be increased to £4,000.'

On page 408, under 'Qualifying investments', sub-paragraphs (*f*)–(*j*) are replaced with the following.

'(*f*)    (Before 6 April 2004) units in, or shares of,

- a securities scheme (broadly an authorised unit trust or open-ended investment company ('OEIC') or part of an umbrella scheme — see 90.1 UNIT TRUSTS), or

- a warrant scheme (broadly a type of authorised unit trust or OEIC investing in warrants or part of an umbrella scheme of that category), or

- a relevant UCITS (an Undertaking for Collective Investment in Transferable Securities situated in and authorised by an EU Member State other than the UK, or part of such an undertaking equivalent to part of an umbrella scheme),

where the scheme or UCITS satisfies the equivalent of the 50% condition in (*e*) above.

# 29   Exempt Income

(*fa*)   (After 5 April 2004) units in, or shares of,

- a securities scheme (as in (*f*) above), or

- a warrant scheme (as in (*f*) above), or

- a relevant UCITS (an Undertaking for Collective Investment in Transferable Securities situated in and authorised by an EU Member State other than the UK, or part of such an undertaking equivalent to part of an umbrella scheme), or

- a fund of funds scheme (as defined),

where the units or shares satisfy the '5% test' outlined below.

(*g*)   (Before 6 April 2004) units in, or shares of, a fund of funds scheme (as defined), subject to the condition that not more than 50% in value of its investments can be investments which would otherwise be within (*f*) above but do not themselves satisfy the 50% condition therein mentioned.

(*ga*)   (After 16 November 2003) units in, or shares of, a Chapter 5 UCITS (an Undertaking for Collective Investment in Transferable Securities complying with Chapter 5 of the Collective Investment Schemes Sourcebook made by the Financial Services Authority) where the units or shares satisfy the '5% test' outlined below.

(*h*)   Shares acquired by the investor under a SAYE share option scheme or all-employee share ownership plan or appropriated to him under an approved profit sharing scheme which are transferred into the ISA as mentioned under '*General*' above.

(*j*)   (From 13 December 2000) a 'depositary interest' in or in relation to an investment which is itself a qualifying investment other than cash. A '*depositary interest*' means the rights of any person to investments held by another, effectively as his nominee. After 16 November 2003 or 5 April 2004 (as appropriate), the underlying investment, if within (*fa*) or (*ga*) above, must satisfy the '5% test' outlined below.'

Immediately after sub-paragraph (*k*) on page 409, the following paragraph is added.

'By concession, a fund of funds scheme that invests in a Chapter 5 UCITS may be eligible for inclusion in an ISA if the Chapter 5 UCITS restricts its investment and borrowing powers to those of a securities scheme (Revenue PEP and ISA Bulletin No 13, 10 December 2003).'

Immediately before the paragraph on page 409 beginning 'Following a revision', the following two paragraphs are added.

'For the purposes of (*fa*), (*ga*) and (*j*) above, an investment satisfies the '*5% test*' if there is no time during the five years after the investment is first held in the ISA when, by virtue of any contract or any other transaction entered into or by virtue of the nature of the underlying investments, the investor is not exposed (or not exposed to any significant extent) to the risk of a loss (from fluctuations in value) exceeding 5% of the sum of the capital consideration paid (or payable) for the acquisition of the investment and the incidental costs of acquisition. Thus, if the investor is certain or near certain of receiving back at least 95% of the investment within five years, for example if he is given a guarantee to that effect or if the scheme or UCITS itself invests substantially in cash, the test is failed.

Investments held in an ISA on 6 April 2004 and within (*f*) or (*g*) above may continue to be held in the ISA notwithstanding the '5% test' introduced in (*fa*) above. The same applies to depositary interests (see (*j*) above) where the underlying investment is within (*f*) or (*g*) above.'

At the foot of page 409, under *Cash Component*, the following three sub-paragraphs are added.

'(vi)   (After 16 November 2003) investments that would fall within (*ga*) above (stocks and shares component) but for their failing the '5% test'.

(vii)   (After 16 November 2003) depositary interests (see (*j*) above) in or in relation to an investment which is itself a qualifying investment for a cash component.

(viii)  (After 5 April 2004) investments that would fall within (*fa*) above (stocks and shares component) but for their failing the '5% test'.'

To the list of statutory references after the first paragraph on page 411, *SI 2003 No 2747* is added.

# 34   Herd Basis

The reference at the head of the chapter to the Revenue Inspector's Manual is replaced by a reference to Revenue Business Income Manual BIM 55501–55640.

# 35   Inland Revenue: Administration

35.9   **Revenue Adjudicator.** The full text is replaced with the following.

'**Adjudicator's Office.** A taxpayer who is not satisfied with the Revenue response to a complaint has the option of putting the case to an independent Adjudicator for the Inland Revenue. The Adjudicator's Office considers complaints about the Revenue's handling of a taxpayer's affairs, e.g. mistakes, delays, misleading advice, staff behaviour or the exercise of Revenue discretion. Matters subject to existing rights of appeal are excluded.

The Adjudicator also investigates complaints about Customs and Excise and the Valuation Office Agency.

The address is The Adjudicator's Office, Haymarket House, 28 Haymarket, London SW1Y 4SP (tel. 020-7930 2292, e-mail address: adjudicators@gtnet.gov.uk).

Complaints normally go to the Adjudicator only after they have been considered by, firstly, the Customer Relations or Complaints Manager and, secondly, the Director of the relevant Revenue office, and where the taxpayer is still not satisfied with the response received. The alternatives of pursuing the complaint to the Revenue's Head Office, to an MP, or (through an MP) to the Parliamentary Ombudsman continue to be available. The Adjudicator reviews all the facts, considers whether the complaint is justified, and, if so, settles the complaint by mediation or makes recommendations as to what should be done. The Revenue normally accept the recommendations.

The Adjudicator publishes an annual report to the Board.

See also Revenue leaflet AO1 'The Adjudicator's Office'.

Leave to apply for judicial review of the rejection by the Adjudicator of a complaint concerning the use of information from unidentified informants was refused in *R v Revenue Adjudicator's Office (ex p Drummond) QB 1996, 70 TC 235*.'

35.12  **Use of electronic communications.** After the second paragraph, the following paragraph is added.

'From 1 January 2004, regulations (*SI 2003 No 3143*) provide for electronic delivery of dividend vouchers, interest vouchers and other tax deduction certificates by prior agreement between sender and recipient.'

35.13    **International co-operation.** In the fourth paragraph, it is noted that relevant Treasury regulations have now been enacted — as *SI 2004 No 674*.

## 37 Inland Revenue Explanatory Publications

The following updated publications are included in the list:

IR 1            Extra-Statutory Concessions as at 31 August 2003 (December 2003).

IR 40(CIS)    Construction Industry Scheme: Conditions for Getting Sub-contractor's Tax Certificate (July 2003).

IR 64          Giving to Charity by Businesses (February 2004).

IR 65          Giving to Charity by Individuals (February 2004).

IR 110        Bank and Building Society Interest — A Guide for Savers (December 2003).

IR 117(CIS) A Guide for Subcontractors with Registration Cards (November 2003).

IR 121        Income Tax and Pensioners (September 2003).

IR 131        Statements of Practice as at 31 August 2003 (February 2004).

IR 170        Blind Person's Allowance (November 2003).

IR 178        Giving Shares and Securities to Charity (February 2004).

IR 2004      Setting up a Charity in Scotland (October 2003).

CGT 1        Capital Gains Tax — An Introduction (December 2003).

AO1          The Adjudicator's Office (September 2003).

COP 9        Special Compliance Office Investigations — Cases of Suspected Serious Fraud (December 2003).

The first paragraph on page 454 is replaced with the following.

"Appeals and Other Proceedings before the Special Commissioners', dealing with procedural and other points, is available free of charge from the Clerk to the Special Commissioners, 15/29 Bedford Avenue, London WC1B 3AS (tel. 020-7631 4242) and at www.financeandtaxtribunals.gov.uk There is also a supplement available on 'IR35 Appeals'.

## 38    Inland Revenue Extra-Statutory Concessions

The following new concession is added.

A103    **Approved employee share schemes: armed forces reservists.** From 7 January 2003, Armed Forces Reservists called up to active service are enabled to maintain their participation in their civilian employers' approved share schemes during the period they are away on service. See 82.2 SHARE-RELATED EMPLOYMENT INCOME AND EXEMPTIONS.

# 39    Inland Revenue Press Releases

The following news releases are added.

8.9.03    **Recovery of tax paid under mistake of law.** Under legislation to be included in *FA 2004*, *Limitation Act 1980, s 32(1)(c)* does *not* apply in relation to a mistake of law relating to taxes administered by the Revenue where the action for restitution is brought on or after today. See 56.11A PAYMENT OF TAX.

6.11.03    **Manufactured dividends on shares acquired under a repo or stock lending arrangement.** New anti-avoidance legislation is to be introduced in *FA 2004* and backdated to today. See 3.7 ANTI-AVOIDANCE.

20.11.03    **Recovery of tax paid under mistake of law.** An amendment is announced to the legislation proposed in the press release of 8 September 2003 above. See 56.11A PAYMENT OF TAX.

10.12.03    **Employer-supported childcare.** From 6 April 2005, an exemption from the employment-related benefit rules is to be introduced for employer-contracted childcare, or childcare vouchers, worth up to £50 per week. See 75.16(xvii) SCHEDULE E — EMPLOYMENT INCOME.

12.1.04    **Official rate of interest on beneficial loans.** This is set in advance at 5% for the tax year 2004/05. See 75.20 SCHEDULE E—EMPLOYMENT INCOME.

15.1.04    **Anti-avoidance: losses on strips of government securities.** With effect from today, legislation in *FA 2004* will block avoidance schemes designed to create artificial losses. See 72.2 SCHEDULE D, CASE III.

30.1.04    **First-year allowances on plant and machinery.** New definitions of 'small or medium-sized enterprise' and 'small enterprise' come into effect. See 10.27 CAPITAL ALLOWANCES.

10.2.04    **Partnership trading losses etc. — anti-avoidance.** Under legislation to be included in *FA 2004*, effective from today, relief against total income or gains, claimed by a partner who does not spend a significant amount of time in running the trade, for losses sustained in any of the first four tax years for which he is a partner cannot exceed the amount contributed to the trade by that partner. The same applies to interest relief claimed by partners against total income. An exit charge is also introduced where such partners have claimed relief for losses derived from expenditure incurred in carrying out an agreement and any rights to receive income under the agreement are disposed of in such a way as to escape a charge to income tax. See 53.10 PARTNERSHIPS.

3.3.04    **Life assurance policies, annuity contracts etc. — deficiency relief.** Under legislation to be included in *FA 2004*, for policies made or entered into (or assigned or becoming security for a debt or into which further premiums are paid) on or after today, any deficiency relief due cannot exceed the aggregate amount of earlier gains on the policy that formed part of the individual's total income for previous tax years. See 45.15 LIFE ASSURANCE POLICIES.

# 40    Inland Revenue Statements of Practice

The following Statements of Practice are added.

SP 2/03    **Business by telephone — non-Contact Centre taxpayers.** Details are given of the services available by telephone from tax offices not served by a Contact Centre. Replaces SP 2/98. See 17.5 CLAIMS.

## 41   Interest on Overpaid Tax

SP 3/03   **Business by telephone — Contact Centre taxpayers.** Details are given of the services available by telephone from Revenue Contact Centres. Replaces SP 8/98. See 17.5 CLAIMS, 67.4 RETURNS .

SP A7 is now incorporated into SP A6 and is therefore deleted.

SP 5/84 now refers to general earnings chargeable under *ITEPA 2003, ss 25, 26* rather than to liability under Schedule E, Cases II and III. SP 3/96 now refers to *ITEPA 2003, ss 225, 226* rather than to *ICTA 1988, s 312.*

## 41   Interest on Overpaid Tax

41.1   **1996/97 onwards (self-assessment).** The following entries are added to the list of rates.

1.75% p.a.      from 6 August 2003 to 5 December 2003
**2.5% p.a.      from 6 December 2003**

41.2   **1995/96 and earlier years.** Identical additions are made as in 41.1 above.

## 42   Interest and Surcharges on Unpaid Tax

42.1   **1996/97 onwards (self-assessment) and assessments raised after 5 April 1998.** The following entries are added to the list of rates.

5.5% p.a.      from 6 August 2003 to 5 December 2003
**6.5% p.a.      from 6 December 2003**

42.2   **Assessments for 1995/96 and earlier years raised before 6 April 1998.** Identical additions are made as in 42.1 above.

## 45   Life Assurance Policies

45.12   **Qualifying policies — Notes.** In sub-paragraph (*d*), immediately before the final paragraph, the following paragraph is added.

'The transfer under a Court Order (between spouses as part of a divorce settlement) of the rights conferred by a policy is regarded as being for no consideration, and thus the policy may continue to attract life assurance premium relief. This represents a change of interpretation of the law by the Revenue, announced initially on their website on 4 November 2003. For full detail, and advice on claiming relief withheld in accordance with the previous interpretation, see Revenue Tax Bulletin December 2003 p 1073.'

45.13   **Life assurance gains.** Immediately before the paragraph headed 'Non-residents' on page 533, the following paragraph is added.

'**Divorce settlements.** The transfer under a Court Order (between spouses as part of a divorce settlement) of the rights conferred by a life policy etc. is not regarded as being for money or money's worth, and thus no taxable gain can arise. This represents a change of interpretation of the law by the Revenue, announced initially on their website on 4 November

2003. For full detail, and advice on amending tax returns prepared in accordance with the previous interpretation, see Revenue Tax Bulletin December 2003 pp 1071–1073.'

45.15    **Partial surrenders etc.** In sub-paragraph (*b*), at the end of the second paragraph, the following is added.

'For policies made or entered into (or assigned or becoming security for a debt or into which further premiums are paid) after 2 March 2004, the amount of such deficiency relief due to an individual cannot exceed the aggregate amount of earlier gains on the policy that formed part of the same individual's total income for tax purposes for previous tax years (Revenue Press Release 3 March 2004).'

# 46    Losses

46.5    **Set-off of trading losses etc. against capital gains.** At the end of the second paragraph, the reference to the Revenue Inspector's Manual is replaced by a reference to Revenue Business Income Manual BIM 75425.

46.8    **Restrictions on above reliefs.** In the penultimate paragraph of sub-paragraph (*a*), the reference to the Revenue Inspector's Manual is replaced by a reference to Revenue Business Income Manual BIM 75705–75725.

The final paragraph of sub-paragraph (*b*) is replaced with the following.

'The Revenue concessionally extend the five-year time limits above to eleven years from commencement in the case of stud farming, i.e. the breeding of thoroughbred horses, provided that the business is potentially profitable (Revenue Business Income Manual BIM 55725).'

In sub-paragraph (*c*), the reference to the Revenue Inspector's Manual is replaced by a reference to Revenue Business Income Manual BIM 75730.

At the end, the following new sub-paragraph is added as sub-paragraph (*f*).

'**Losses derived from film tax reliefs.** New anti-avoidance legislation was announced in the December 2003 Pre-Budget Report and is aimed at individuals who have contributed to the cost of a film, have leased back the film by way of trade (usually in partnership) to the filmmakers, have claimed relief under *ICTA 1988, s 380* (or under *ICTA 1988, s 381* — see 46.13 below) for losses derived from the accelerated film tax reliefs at 71.58 SCHEDULE D, CASES I AND II and who effect a complete or partial 'exit' after 9 December 2003. An '*exit*' occurs where the individual disposes of, gives up, or otherwise loses, all or part of the right to receive income from the leaseback or similar arrangement before the completion of its specified term in such a way as to obtain consideration that would otherwise be free of income tax and/or to obtain relief for losses greater than the economic losses actually borne by him. The loss relief itself is not withdrawn, but taxable income is deemed to arise in the tax year of exit, based on the consideration received and, if any, the difference between losses relieved and losses ultimately borne. The legislation will be in *FA 2004* and is in response to marketed exit schemes. For more detail and for examples, see the document 'Avoidance using exits from businesses that have accessed film tax reliefs' included as part of the 2003 Pre-Budget Report material on the Revenue website.'

46.10    **Notes.** The last two sentences of sub-paragraph (*b*) are replaced with the following.

'See further Revenue Business Income Manual BIM 75225, 75230. See also BIM 75220 as regards changes to claims.'

46.12    **Losses carried forward.** In sub-paragraph (*c*), the reference to the Revenue Inspector's Manual is replaced by a reference to Revenue Business Income Manual BIM 75500.

# 51    Non-Residents and other Overseas Matters

46.13    **Losses in early years of a trade.** In the opening paragraph, immediately after the reference to *Walls v Livesey*, there is added a reference to *Walsh and Another v Taylor (Sp C 386) 2003, [2004] SSCD 48.*

In the notes that follow, it is noted that the anti-avoidance legislation at 46.8(*f*) above (losses derived from film tax reliefs) applies equally where the loss relief is claimed under *ICTA 1988, s 381.*

# 51    Non-Residents and other Overseas Matters

51.6    **Persons not treated as UK representatives for tax purposes.** At the end, passing reference is made to *SI 2003 No 2172.*

51.8    **Non-resident entertainers and sportsmen.** At the end of the second paragraph, the following sentence is added.

'See *Set, Deuce and Ball v Robinson (Sp C 373), [2003] SSCD 382* which analysed this definition in relation to non-resident tennis players performing at Wimbledon (and in which it was also held that payments *by* non-residents *to* non-residents are within these provisions).'

# 53    Partnerships

53.2    **Nature of partnership.** A third of the way down page 613, the reference to the Revenue Inspector's Manual is replaced by a reference to Revenue Business Income Manual BIM 72001–72035.

53.10    **Losses.** After the second full paragraph on page 630, the following is added.

'**Anti-avoidance.** Under legislation to be included in *FA 2004*, effective for losses derived from expenditure incurred after 9 February 2004, relief under *ICTA 1988, s 380, FA 1991, s 72* or *ICTA 1988, s 381* (see, respectively, 46.3, 46.5, 46.13 LOSSES) against total income or gains, claimed by a partner who does not spend a 'significant' amount of time in running the trade, for trading losses sustained in any of the first four tax years in which he carries on the partnership trade cannot exceed the amount contributed to the trade by that partner. A similar rule applies to interest relief claimed by partners under *ICTA 1988, s 353* (see 43.3 INTEREST PAYABLE) against total income. Any amount remaining unrelieved can be carried forward to the following year (but the same restriction applies for that year) or (in the case of a loss) can be carried forward against income of the trade in subsequent years under *ICTA 1988, s 385* (see 46.12 LOSSES). The restriction operates after applying any other rules that restrict loss relief or interest relief. A '*significant*' amount of time is regarded as a minimum of ten hours per week, taken across the period as a whole. It includes only time spent in playing an active and personal role in the operations of the trade. This excludes time spent considering information to decide whether and how much to invest in a trade, considering reports and information provided by others about the progress of a trade and taking decisions concerning the trade based on such information. The restriction does not affect the underwriting activities of UNDERWRITERS AT LLOYD's (89) and does not apply to limited partners and members of LLPs (for which see the special rules below).

Also for losses derived from expenditure incurred after 9 February 2004, an exit charge applies as described below where all the following conditions are met:

- an individual has claimed relief, under *ICTA 1988, s 380, FA 1991, s 72* or *ICTA 1988, s 381* against total income or gains, for losses incurred in any of the first four years of a trade in which he is a partner;

- he did not spend a 'significant' amount of time in running the trade (see above) in the year when the losses were incurred;

- the losses derive from expenditure incurred in carrying out an agreement, and any rights to receive income under that agreement are disposed of in such a way as to escape an income tax charge; and

- the total losses so claimed in those first four years exceed the cumulative profits arising to the partner concerned since he commenced in the trade.

An income charge arises on the lesser of the disposal proceeds not otherwise chargeable to income tax and the excess of losses claimed over cumulative profits. Where there is a series of part disposals of rights, the cumulative position is taken into account. Once the loss relief is 'exhausted', no subsequent adjustment to the exit charge can be made for later years' profits. Related or connected agreements are treated as a single agreement.

(Revenue Press Release and Internet Statement 10 February 2004).'

A third of the way down page 631, the reference to the Revenue Inspector's Manual is replaced by a reference to Revenue Business Income Manual BIM 72101–72105.

At the foot of page 631, the following paragraph is added.

'With effect on and after 10 February 2004, under legislation to be included in *FA 2004*, a member of a trading LLP who does not spend a 'significant' amount of time in running the trade (for which see above under 'Anti-avoidance) can claim relief against total income or gains under *ICTA 1988, s 380, FA 1991, s 72* or *ICTA 1988, s 381* (see, respectively, 46.3, 46.5, 46.13 LOSSES) only up to an amount equal to that which he contributes to the LLP, either during the course of a trade or in a winding-up. A similar rule applies to interest relief claimed by members of LLPs under *ICTA 1988, s 353* (see 43.3 INTEREST PAYABLE) against total income. (Revenue Internet Statement 10 February 2004).'

53.13    **Spouse as partner.** The full text is replaced with the following.

'Where a spouse is taken into partnership, perhaps to maximise the benefit of personal reliefs and rate bands, the Revenue cannot challenge the apportionment of profits as they could the payment of a salary to a spouse. There is no requirement for the spouse to contribute capital or to participate in management or even to take an active part in the business. Note, however, the possible application of the settlements legislation at *ICTA 1988, s 660A* where one spouse takes the other into partnership with a share of profits but with no requirement, or insufficient requirement, to contribute capital and/or personal time and effort (see 81.16(*a*) SETTLEMENTS and Revenue Tax Bulletin April 2003 pp 1011–1016). See also Revenue Business Income Manual BIM 72065, which, as well as discussing the above, also covers the less frequent event of minor children being taken into partnership.'

# 55    Pay As You Earn

55.1    **Introduction.** At the end of the second paragraph, it is noted that the rewritten PAYE regulations were published in October 2003 as *SI 2003 No 2682* and take effect on 6 April 2004. All references to the superseded regulations will be updated in the 2004/05 main edition. Some have been updated below in advance of their coming into effect.

# 55 Pay As You Earn

55.2    **Scope of PAYE.** In sub-paragraph (*a*), reference is made to Revenue Employment Income Manual EIM 11900 for further notes on the meaning of 'readily convertible assets'. In sub-paragraphs (*f*) and (*h*), it is noted that the appointed day was 1 September 2003 as expected — by virtue of *SI 2003 No 1997*.

55.8    **Tax deducted under PAYE to be paid over to the Revenue.** The final paragraph is replaced with the following.

'**Mandatory electronic payment for 'large employers'.** For 2004/05 and subsequent years, employers who at the 'specified date' were 'large employers' (i.e. they were paying PAYE income to at least 250 recipients) are required, upon receipt of an e-payment notice issued by the Revenue by 31 December in the tax year preceding the year of payment, to use an approved method of electronic payment of PAYE liabilities. An appeal may be made (within 30 days) against an e-payment notice on the grounds that the employer is not a 'large employer'. In relation to 2004/05, the '*specified date*' is 26 October 2003. A system of default surcharges, ranging from 0.17% to 0.83% of the annual net PAYE liability, applies for persistent failure to make payments in full by the due dates; a person is not in default if he has a reasonable excuse (excluding inability to pay). Appeals may be made against default notices and surcharge notices. [*FA 2003, ss 204, 205; SI 2003 No 2682, regs 190, 191, 199–204; Revenue Direction 21 October 2003*]. See also Revenue Tax Bulletin February 2004 p 1085.'

It is also noted that the 14-day period after the end of each tax month within which PAYE payments must be made to the Revenue is extended to 17 days where payments are made electronically for 2004/05 onwards.

55.9    **Action at end of tax year.** The penultimate and ante-penultimate paragraphs (page 648) are replaced with the following.

'**Mandatory e-filing.** The Commissioners of Inland Revenue have been given extremely wide powers to make regulations requiring the use of electronic communications for the delivery of information required or authorised to be delivered under tax legislation. [*FA 2002, ss 135, 136*]. The Government has adopted a three-stage move towards e-filing of PAYE returns (i.e. the information required at (*a*) above), as follows.

(A)    Employers with 250 or more employees are required to file electronically from 2004/05.

(B)    Employers with 50 or more employees are required to file electronically from 2005/06.

(C)    Employers with less than 50 employees are required to file electronically from 2009/10, with an incentive for earlier adoption.

(Revenue/C&E Budget Press Release 2/02, 17 April 2002).

Under the regulations giving effect to (A) and (B) above, the mandatory e-filing requirement applies for 2004/05 to employers who at 26 October 2003 were 'large employers' (i.e. they were paying PAYE income to at least 250 recipients) and who received an e-filing notice issued by the Revenue no later than 31 December 2003. Similar provisions apply for subsequent years but by reference to employers who at the specified date (to be announced by Revenue Direction) were 'large or medium-sized employers' (i.e. they were paying PAYE income to at least 50 recipients) and who received an e-filing notice issued by the Revenue no later than 31 December preceding the tax year in question. An appeal may be made (within 30 days) against an e-filing notice on the grounds that the employer does not fall into the specified category. There are let-outs for members of any religious orders whose beliefs are incompatible with electronic communication. Penalties for failure to comply range from £600 to £3,000 depending upon the number of employees, the maximum penalty applying where there are 1,000 or more. Appeals may be made against penalty determinations on specified grounds including reasonable excuse throughout the default period. [*SI 2003 No 2682, regs 190, 191, 205–210; Revenue Direction 21 October 2003*].

Regulations have also been made to give effect to (C) above. The incentives are available to employers who at a specified date (to be announced by Revenue Direction) preceding the tax year in question were 'small employers' (i.e. they were paying PAYE income to less than 50 recipients) or who first started paying PAYE income after that date. The payments receivable are £250 for each of 2004/05 and 2005/06, £150 for 2006/07, £100 for 2007/08 and £75 for 2008/09. These are not chargeable to tax. Appeals are possible (within 30 days of the notice) against an officer's decision not to make an incentive payment or to recover a payment already made. [*SI 2003 No 2495; Revenue Direction 21 October 2003*]. Employers can either use incentive payments to reduce a subsequent PAYE liability or claim a repayment, but repayments will not be sent to the employer's agent (Revenue Tax Bulletin February 2004 p 1085).

See also Revenue Tax Bulletins February 2003 pp 995, 996, February 2004 pp 1084, 1085.

**Mandatory e-payment for 'large employers'.** See 55.8 above.'

55.18    **Crown priority.** It is noted that the abolition of Crown priority by *Enterprise Act 2002, s 251* took effect from 15 September 2003 (per *SI 2003 No 2093*).

55.42    **Tips, organised arrangements for sharing.** The full text is replaced with the following.

'Gratuities and service charge shares under such arrangements (sometimes known as a 'tronc') are within PAYE and the 'troncmaster' (i.e. the person running the arrangements, being a person other than the employer) is regarded as responsible for the tax deductions. For arrangements coming into existence after 5 April 2004, the employer, on becoming aware of their existence, must notify the Revenue and give the name of the person running them, if known. [*ITEPA 2003, s 692; SI 2003 No 2682, reg 100*]. For a case in which informal arrangements, under which directors of the employing company collected gratuities and divided them between themselves and the employees, were held not to constitute organised arrangements, see *Figael Ltd v Fox CA 1991, 64 TC 441*.

The above rules apply where the troncmaster acts independently of the employer. If the employer himself acts as troncmaster, or appoints an employee to make distributions in accordance with the employer's own formula or is otherwise involved in the distribution of monies from the tronc, payments made under the arrangements must be dealt with through the employer's own PAYE system. (Revenue Tax Bulletin February 2004 p 1081).

See generally Revenue Employment Procedures Manual EP 1155 *et seq.*, Revenue booklet E24 'Tips, Gratuities, Service Charges and Troncs: A Guide to Income Tax, National Insurance contributions, National Minimum Wage issues and VAT' (distributed to employers) and Revenue Tax Bulletin February 2004 pp 1081–1084.'

# 56    Payment of Tax

56.8    **Crown priority.** It is noted that the abolition of the remaining Crown priority by *Enterprise Act 2002, s 251* took effect from 15 September 2003 (per *SI 2003 No 2093*).

56.11A    **Recovery of tax paid under mistake of law.** New text is added as follows.

'It was held in *R v CIR (ex p. Woolwich Equitable Building Society) HL 1990, 63 TC 589* that at common law taxes extracted *ultra vires* are recoverable as of right and without need to invoke mistake of law by the taxpayer (and see 41.3 INTEREST ON OVERPAID TAX).

It was further held, *inter alia*, in *Deutsche Morgan Grenfell Group plc v CIR and A-G Ch D, [2003] STC 1017* that the common law remedy of restitution of payment made under a mistake of law applies to payments of tax as it does to other payments. By virtue of *Limitation Act 1980, s 32(1)(c)*, the six-year period of limitation in such a case does not begin to run until the plaintiff discovers the mistake (or could with reasonable diligence have discovered it). However, under legislation to be included in *FA 2004* (reversing the effect of *Deutsche Morgan Grenfell*), *Limitation Act 1980, s 32(1)(c)* (and Scottish equivalent) does *not* apply in relation to a mistake of law relating to taxes administered by the Inland Revenue where the action for restitution is brought **after 7 September 2003**. The effect is that court actions for restitution based on mistake of law must generally be brought within six years (or five years under Scottish law) of the tax having been paid. If, after 19 November 2003, a pre-existing action is amended to include additional years, the amendment is no longer treated as backdated to the date of the original action. (Revenue Press Releases 8 September 2003, 20 November 2003).'

# 57    Penalties

57.2    **Failure to make timeous return.** The last paragraph on page 663 is replaced with the following.

'The Revenue's original intention was to use the daily penalty sanction above where the tax at risk was substantial and they believed the fixed penalties to be an insufficient deterrent (Revenue booklet SAT 2 (1995), para 2.74 (now out of print)), but they have since stated that they will be increasing their use of such sanctions. (Revenue Tax Bulletins February 2002 p 915, December 2003 p 1067).'

# 66    Retirement Schemes for Employees

66.4    **Conditions for approval after 5 April 1973.** The final paragraph of sub-paragraph (*c*) is replaced with the following.

"Retirement' in (i) above means retirement from the service of the company whether as an employee or as a director but not necessarily from both positions; an individual who retired from paid employment but continued as an unpaid non-executive director was held by the HL to have duly retired and to have been entitled to receive payments from the company's pension scheme (*Venables and Others v Hornby HL 2003, [2004] STC 84*).'

# 67    Returns

67.2    **Annual returns of income and chargeable gains under self-assessment.** In the paragraph headed 'Accounts' on page 766, the reference to Revenue booklet SAT 2 is replaced by a reference to Revenue Income Tax Self-Assessment: The Legal Framework Manual SALF 203, paras 2.18, 2.19.

67.3    **Self-assessments.** In the final paragraph, the reference to Revenue booklet SAT 2 is replaced by a reference to Revenue Income Tax Self-Assessment: The Legal Framework Manual SALF 204, para 2.33.

67.4    **Amendments of returns other than where enquiries made.** Immediately before the final paragraph, the following paragraph is added.

'Individuals whose tax office is served by a Call Centre may notify certain amendments by telephone (Revenue Statement of Practice SP 3/03, 1 September 2003). See also 17.5 CLAIMS.'

67.16    **Bankers etc. and paying agents — returns of interest.** In the paragraph headed 'EU Directive on the Taxation of Savings', it is noted that *SI 2003 No 3297 (Reporting of Savings Income Information Regulations 2003)* has now been enacted. These regulations implement part of the Directive but will not take effect any earlier than 1 January 2005. See Revenue Internet Statement 19 December 2003. The regulations prescribe the types of paying agent and payee within the scheme, the information required, the time limits for compliance and the penalties for non-compliance, and it provides for inspection of paying agents' records. For these purposes, '*savings income*' means interest (including premium bond winnings but not interest unrelated to a money debt or penalty charges for late payments), interest accrued or capitalised at the sale, refund or redemption of a money debt, and certain income distributed by or realised upon the sale, refund or redemption of shares or units in a collective investment fund. See the Revenue's detailed Savings Income Reporting Guidance Notes at www.inlandrevenue.gov.uk/esd-guidance/esd-guidance-notes.pdf    and www.inlandrevenue.gov.uk/esd-guidance/contractualrelations.pdf

# 68    Schedule A — Property Income

68.9    **Furnished holiday lettings.** On page 791, the text between sub-paragraph (*b*) at the top of the page and sub-paragraph (1) is replaced with the following.

'It must, however, not normally be in the same occupation for more than 31 consecutive days at any time during a period (although not necessarily a continuous period) of seven months in that twelve month period which includes any months in which it is let as in (*b*) above. The words 'in the same occupation' refer to tenants and do not prevent relief being due where the owner himself occupies the property outside the holiday season (Revenue Property Income Manual PIM 4110).

In the case of an individual or partnership, these conditions must be satisfied in the year of assessment in which the profits or gains arise, unless'

68.11    **'Rent a room' relief.** In the first full paragraph on page 793, the reference to the Revenue Inspector's Manual is replaced by a reference to Revenue Property Income Manual PIM 4050.

The last two paragraphs on page 793 are replaced with the following.

'A '*qualifying residence*' is a 'residence' which is the individual's only or main residence at any time in the basis period for the year of assessment in relation to the source in question. The furnished accommodation let within the qualifying residence may be in a self-contained flat provided that the division into a self-contained unit is only temporary (Revenue Property Income Manual PIM 4004).

'*Residence*' means a building (or part) occupied or intended to be occupied as a separate residence (ignoring any temporary division into separate residences of a building (or part) designed for permanent use as a single residence), or a caravan or house-boat.

'Rent a room' relief will not normally be available to taxpayers who are living abroad (or in job-related accommodation) and letting their home while they are away; this applies even in the years of departure and return since the property will not normally have been their residence at any time during the basis periods for those years. If, however, the letting commences *before* departure and/or ceases *after* return, relief may then be due for the year of departure and/or return. (Revenue Property Income Manual PIM 4010, 4015).'

68.28    **Premiums etc. on leases of up to 50 years — allowance to payer.** In the first line, the reference to the Revenue Inspector's Manual is replaced by a reference to Revenue Property Income Manual PIM 2300–2340.

# 71    Schedule D, Cases I and II

**71.32**    **Futures, options and swap contracts.** The full text is replaced with the following.

'As far as companies are concerned, almost all futures, options and swaps fall within the derivative contracts rules applicable for accounting periods beginning on or after 1 October 2002 (see Tolley's Corporation Tax under Financial Instruments and derivative contracts), so the following now applies mainly for income tax purposes.

**Futures and options.** Any gain arising in the course of dealing, other than in the course of trade, in commodity or financial futures or in traded or financial options on a recognised exchange, and not chargeable under *ICTA 1988, Sch 5AA* (see 3.22 ANTI-AVOIDANCE), is dealt with under the chargeable gains rules and is not chargeable to tax under Schedule D. [*ICTA 1988, s 128; TCGA 1992, s 143; FA 1994, s 95; FA 1997, s 80(3); FA 2002, Sch 27 para 3*]. See Tolley's Capital Gains Tax under Disposal.

Where dealing is in the course of a trade, any profit or loss is chargeable under Schedule D, Case I. In general, relatively infrequent transactions, and transactions to hedge specific investments, would not be regarded as trading, nor would purely speculative transactions. For the Revenue view on what constitutes trading in this context, see Revenue Pamphlet IR 131, SP 3/02 (replacing SP 14/91).

Special rules are applied (by regulation) to the market formed by the merger of the London International Financial Futures Exchange (LIFFE) and the London Traded Options Market (LTOM), which operates outside the Stock Exchange. These relate to bond-washing and to stamp duty and stamp duty reserve tax. See *SI 1992 Nos 568, 570.*

*Pension schemes etc.* For the purposes of approved retirement benefit schemes (see 66.5(*b*), 66.13 RETIREMENT SCHEMES), personal pension schemes and retirement annuity trust schemes (see 59.1 PERSONAL PENSION SCHEMES, 65.8 RETIREMENT ANNUITIES), futures and options contracts are treated as investments (and thus as attracting tax exemption for income and capital gains). Any income derived from transactions relating to such a contract is regarded as arising from the contract, and a contract is not excluded from these provisions by the fact that any party is, or may be, entitled to receive and/or liable to make only a payment of a sum in full settlement of all obligations, as opposed to a transfer of assets other than money. [*ICTA 1988, s 659A; TCGA 1992, s 271(10)(11); FA 1990, s 81(2)(3)(5)(6)*].

**Swaps.** The word 'swap' is not defined for tax purposes but is taken to mean any financial arrangement that would be regarded by the financial markets as a swap. Profits or losses on a swap are within Schedule D, Case I if on trading account and are otherwise within Schedule D, Case VI (if not of a capital nature). When considering whether a swap transaction is within Case I or Case VI, the Revenue apply the general principles set out in Statement of Practice SP 3/02 referred to above, and for an overview see also Revenue Tax Bulletin August 2003 pp 1054, 1055.

*Pension schemes etc. ICTA 1988, s 659A* referred to above has no bearing on the tax status of swaps. Where a swap transaction by an approved scheme falls close to the trading/investment borderline, the Revenue judge the case on its merits. Where an approved scheme uses interest rate swaps, currency swaps, equity swaps, credit derivatives or similar instruments to hedge risks inherent in, or as part of a strategy to enhance the return from, its existing investment portfolio or (in line with its normal policies of investing directly in such investments) to create a synthetic exposure to investments of a particular type or in a particular market, the Revenue normally regard such swaps as investments (and thus as attracting tax exemptions for income and capital gains). (Revenue Tax Bulletin August 2003 pp 1055, 1056).'

**71.37**    **Miscellaneous.** The fourth paragraph is replaced with the following.

'For whether or not an *athlete* is taxable under Case I, see Revenue Business Income Manual BIM 50605; for the treatment of Lottery Sports Fund Athlete Personal Awards, see BIM 50651–50690.'

71.38    **Property transactions.** In the first paragraph, the reference to the Revenue Inspector's Manual is replaced by a reference to Revenue Business Income Manual BIM 60000–60165.

71.40    **General.** The line immediately above 71.40 is replaced with the following.

'See Revenue Business Income Manual BIM 50000 *et seq.* for Revenue guidance on measuring the profits of a wide range of particular trades.'

The first paragraph on page 846 is replaced with the following.

'**True and fair view requirement.** For periods of account (i.e. any period for which accounts of a trade, profession or vocation are drawn up) beginning **after 6 April 1999**, *FA 1998, s 42* provides that the profits of a trade, profession or vocation must generally be computed for tax purposes on an accounting basis giving a true and fair view, subject to any adjustment required or authorised by law. This imposes a general requirement to apply an earnings basis (see below) for tax purposes, whilst at the same time importing the accountancy concept of 'materiality', allowing a practical view to be taken of the time when immaterial amounts are recognised. The 'true and fair view' rule requires neither the auditing of accounts, nor additional disclosure, nor the preparation of a true and fair view balance sheet. Neither does it require accounts to be drawn up on any particular basis (provided the necessary adjustments are made in the tax computation). See Revenue Press Release 17 March 1998. For the Revenue view of what is meant by 'true and fair view', see Revenue Tax Bulletin December 1998 pp 606-615. See Revenue Business Income Manual BIM 31045–31047 as regards the concept of materiality.'

Three-quarters of the way down that page, the reference to the Revenue Inspector's Manual is deleted.

On page 848, the paragraph headed 'Accountancy principles' *and* the following paragraph are replaced with the following.

'**Accountancy principles.** See above as regards the adoption of GAAP in the computation of taxable profits. Even prior to this, it had always been the case that, since the starting figure in computing profits was that brought out by the accounts of the business, accountancy principles were of the greatest importance. They could not, however, override established income tax principles (*Heather v P-E Consulting Group Ltd CA 1972, 48 TC 293*; *Willingale v International Commercial Bank Ltd HL 1977, 52 TC 242*; but see *Threlfall v Jones CA 1993, 66 TC 77*; *Johnston v Britannia Airways Ltd Ch D 1994, 67 TC 99*). See also *RTZ Oil & Gas Ltd v Elliss Ch D 1987, 61 TC 132*. A 'provision for a future operating loss', whose inclusion could not be said to have 'violated existing accounting principles', was disallowed in *Meat Traders Ltd v Cushing (Sp C 131), [1997] SSCD 245*). See *Robertson v CIR (Sp C 137), [1997] SSCD 282* as regards timing of inclusion of insurance agents' advance commission. See also *Herbert Smith v Honour Ch D 1999, 72 TC 130* for the timing of deductions in respect of future rents under leases of premises ceasing to be used for business purposes, and Revenue Press Release 20 July 1999 for Revenue practice following that decision.

Per Sir Thomas Bingham MR in *Threlfall v Jones*: ' … I find it hard to understand how any judge-made rule could override the application of a generally accepted rule of commercial accountancy which (a) applied to the situation in question, (b) was not one of two or more rules applicable to the situation in question and (c) was not shown to be inconsistent with the true facts or otherwise inapt to determine the true profits or losses of the business'. FRS 18 now requires companies to choose accounting policies that are most appropriate to their particular circumstances (see Revenue Tax Bulletin April 2002 p 924).

If an entity has correctly followed an International Accounting Standard or USA standard, which does not conflict with UK GAAP, including the requirements of FRS 18 (accounting policies), and this accurately reflects the facts, the accountancy treatment will comply with the requirement of *FA 1998, s 42* above (Revenue Business Income Manual BIM 31027).

For the Revenue view on the relationship between accountancy and taxable profits, see Revenue Business Income Manual BIM 31000–31120 and Revenue Tax Bulletin December 1997 pp 485, 486, February 1999 pp 623-625, April 1999 pp 636-641, December 1999 pp 707-709, June 2001 pp 859, 860. For generally accepted accounting practice and accounting standards, see BIM 31020–31070. For the timing of deductions where an expense is taken to the balance sheet rather than charged immediately against profits, i.e. *deferred revenue expenditure*, see Revenue Business Income Manual BIM 42215, 42220. For *provisions*, see Revenue Business Income Manual BIM 46500 *et seq.* and Revenue Press Release 20 July 1999, Revenue Tax Bulletin December 1999 pp 707-709.'

On page 849, immediately before the paragraph headed 'Wholly and exclusively', the following paragraph is added.

'For the Revenue's own guidance on capital *v* income, see Revenue Business Income Manual BIM 35000–35910.'

The paragraph headed 'Wholly and exclusively' is replaced with the following.

'**Wholly and exclusively.** Any expense to be deductible must, *inter alia*, have been incurred 'wholly and exclusively ... for the purposes' of the trade etc. *[ICTA 1988, s 74(1)(a)]*. This provision underlies, explicitly or implicitly, the very large number of 'expenses' cases noted in the paragraphs below. For a review of the leading cases see *Harrods (Buenos Aires) Ltd v Taylor-Gooby CA 1964, 41 TC 450* and for a frequently quoted analysis of the words see *Bentleys, Stokes & Lowless v Beeson CA 1952, 33 TC 491*. Since that case the '*dual purpose rule*' has figured prominently in Court decisions. If an expense is for a material private or non-business purpose, the whole is strictly disallowable as it is thereby not wholly and exclusively for business purposes. For examples of its application see 71.74 and 71.90 below. 'Dual expenditure is expenditure that is incurred for more than one reason. If one of the reasons is not for business purposes, the expenditure fails the statutory test and there is no provision that allows a "business" proportion' (Revenue Business Income Manual BIM 37007). *However*, in practice, where an identifiable part or proportion of an expense has been laid out wholly and exclusively for the purposes of the trade, the Revenue do not disallow that part or proportion on the grounds that the expense is not *as a whole* laid out wholly and exclusively for the purposes of the trade (BIM 37007). For rent etc. of premises used both for business and as residence, see 71.78 below.

See *Mallalieu v Drummond* (71.74) for an important HL discussion of *ICTA 1988, s 74(1)(a)*, in which it was held that the purposes of the relevant expenditure involved looking into the taxpayer's mind at the time of the expenditure, later events being irrelevant except as a reflection of that state of mind. However, the taxpayer's conscious motive at the time was not conclusive; an object, not a conscious motive (in this case the human requirement for clothing), could be taken into account.

A purely incidental consequence of a business expense does not, however, preclude its being wholly and exclusively for business purposes (Revenue Business Income Manual BIM 37007, 37400). See, for example, *Robinson v Scott Bader Ltd*, 71.54 below and *McKnight v Sheppard HL 1999, 71 TC 419*, 71.69, 71.74 below. *Mallalieu v Drummond* was applied in *Watkis v Ashford, Sparkes and Harward Ch D 1985, 58 TC 468*, where expenditure on meals supplied at regular partners' lunchtime meetings was disallowed, overruling the Commissioner's finding that the expenditure was exclusively for business purposes. Expenditure on accommodation, food and drink at the firm's annual weekend conference was, however, allowed. For deduction of payments by partnerships to individual partners generally, see *MacKinlay v Arthur Young McClelland Moores & Co HL 1989, 62 TC 704*. Salaries paid to partners are not deductible as trading expenses (*PDC Copyprint (South) v George (Sp C 141), [1997] SSCD 326).*'

On page 850, immediately before the paragraph headed 'Employment income', the following paragraph is added.

'For the Revenue's own guidance on the 'wholly and exclusively' rule, see Revenue Business Income Manual BIM 37000–38600.'

At the end of the paragraph headed 'Private Finance Initiative', a reference is added to Revenue Business Income Manual BIM 64000–64405.

71.41 **Advertising.** The reference to the Revenue Inspector's Manual is replaced by a reference to Revenue Business Income Manual BIM 42550–42555.

71.43 **Artistes.** Immediately before the final paragraph, the following paragraph is added.

'For deductibility of expenses of actors and other entertainers, including clothing, costume, grooming and cosmetic surgery, see Revenue Business Income Manual BIM 50160.'

71.44 **Bad and doubtful debts.** The reference in the first line to the Revenue Inspector's Manual is replaced by a reference to Revenue Business Income Manual BIM 42700–42750. The reference at the end of the third paragraph to the Inspector's Manual is replaced by a reference to Business Income Manual BIM 40201, 42740. The reference at the end of the eighth paragraph to the Inspector's Manual is replaced by a reference to Business Income Manual BIM 42735.

71.49 **Contingent and future liabilities.** The third paragraph (page 858) is replaced with the following.

'No deduction is normally permissible for future repairs or renewals (*Clayton v Newcastle-under-Lyme Corpn QB 1888, 2 TC 416; Naval Colliery Co Ltd v CIR HL 1928, 12 TC 1017; Peter Merchant Ltd v Stedeford CA 1948, 30 TC 496*). However, this rule is now subject to Financial Reporting Standard FRS 12 (see 71.79(*b*) below). No deduction is permissible for the future cost of collecting debts (*Monthly Salaries Loan Co v Furlong Ch D 1962, 40 TC 313*) or for future payments of damages in respect of accidents to employees unless liability has been admitted or established (*James Spencer & Co v CIR CS 1950, 32 TC 111*). See also *Albion Rovers Football Club v CIR HL 1952, 33 TC 331* (wages deductible when paid). A provision for regular major overhaul work accrued due on aircraft engines was allowed in *Johnston v Britannia Airways Ltd Ch D 1994, 67 TC 99* (but see now Revenue Tax Bulletin February 1999 p 624 and further below as regards changes in accounting practice superseding this decision).'

The reference in the final paragraph to the Revenue Inspector's Manual is replaced by a reference to Revenue Business Income Manual BIM 42201, 46500–46565.

71.51 **Creative artists.** The third paragraph is replaced with the following.

'Whether a literary prize or award is a receipt of the author's profession depends on the precise facts, see Revenue Business Income Manual BIM 50710, 50715.'

71.54 **Employees (and directors).** The decision in *Macdonald v Dextra Accessories*, noted on pages 864 and 868 has been reversed by the Court of Appeal, which ruled in favour of the Revenue (see *2004 STI 234*).

In sub-paragraph (*e*) at the top of page 867, the reference to the Revenue Inspector's Manual is replaced by a reference to Revenue Business Income Manual BIM 44025. In the immediately following paragraph, the reference to the Inspector's Manual is replaced by a reference to Business Income Manual BIM 44030.

Immediately before the paragraph headed 'Counselling services etc.' on page 869, the reference to the Revenue Inspector's Manual is replaced by a reference to Revenue Business Income Manual BIM 46600–46615.

In the paragraph headed 'Key employee insurance' (page 869), the reference to the Revenue Inspector's Manual is replaced by a reference to Revenue Business Income Manual BIM 45525, 45530 and the following sentence is added.

'In *Greycon Ltd v Klaentschi (Sp C 372), [2003] SSCD 370*, it was held that the company's sole purpose in taking out key man policies was to meet a requirement of an agreement under which funding and other benefits were obtained from another company, that the policies had a capital purpose and that, consequently, the proceeds were not trading receipts.'

71.55    **Entertainment expenses.** At the end, the reference to the Revenue Inspector's Manual is replaced by a reference to Revenue Business Income Manual BIM 45000–45090.

71.57    **Farming and market gardening.** In sub-paragraph (*a*) (averaging of profits), the reference at the foot of page 876 to the Revenue Inspector's Manual is replaced by a reference to Revenue Business Income Manual BIM 73000–73190.

In sub-paragraph (*b*) (compulsory slaughter) (page 877), the reference to the Revenue Inspector's Manual is replaced by a reference to Revenue Business Income Manual BIM 55185.

In sub-paragraph (*d*) (farmhouses) (page 877), the reference at the end to the Revenue Inspector's Manual is replaced by a reference to Revenue Business Income Manual BIM 75610.

At the end of the text (page 880), the reference to the Revenue Inspector's Manual is replaced by a reference to Revenue Business Income Manual BIM 55000–55730, 73000–73190 and 75600–75650.

71.58    **Film production.** In line 2, the reference to guidance on the Revenue website is replaced by a reference to Revenue Business Income Manual BIM 56000–56530.

71.59    **Franchising.** The reference at the end to the Revenue Inspector's Manual is replaced by a reference to Revenue Business Income Manual BIM 57600–57620. The following paragraph is then added.

'For *companies* acquiring and selling franchises after 31 March 2002, the intangible assets regime (see Tolley's Corporation Tax under Intangible Assets) is likely to apply and takes precedence over the above.'

71.60    **Gifts and other non-contractual receipts and payments.** At the end of the paragraph headed 'Cremation fees' (page 885), the reference to the Revenue Inspector's Manual is replaced by a reference to Revenue Business Income Manual BIM 54015.

71.62    **Hire-purchase.** The reference at the end to the Revenue Inspector's Manual is replaced by references to Revenue Business Income Manual BIM 40550–40555 (hire-purchase receipts) and BIM 45350–45365 (hire-purchase payments).

71.63    **Illegal payments.** The reference at the end to the Revenue Inspector's Manual is replaced by a reference to Revenue Business Income Manual BIM 43100–43185.

71.64    **Insurance.** At the end of the first full paragraph on page 887, the following sentence is added.

'In *Greycon Ltd v Klaentschi (Sp C 372), [2003] SSCD 370*, it was held that the company's sole purpose in taking out key man policies was to meet a requirement of an agreement under which funding and other benefits were obtained from another company, that the policies had a capital purpose and that, consequently, the proceeds were not trading receipts.'

The paragraph headed 'Locum and fixed practice expenses insurance' is replaced with the following.

'With effect for periods of account beginning after 30 September 1996, the Revenue take the view that premiums for such policies are deductible, and benefits taxable, under Schedule D, Case II, whether the professional person is obliged to insure (e.g. under NHS regulations) or does so as a matter of commercial prudence. This view relates to premiums paid by professional people such as doctors and dentists to meet locum and/or fixed overhead costs. It does not apply to any part of a premium relating to other, non-business, risks such as the cost of medical treatment for accident or sickness. (Revenue Press Release 30 April 1996).'

71.68    **Lease rental payments.** In the third paragraph, the case citation is changed to *Lloyds UDT Finance Ltd and Another v Britax International GmBH and Another CA 2002, 74 TC 662.*

On page 891, at the end of the text on Finance lease rentals, the reference to the Revenue Inspector's Manual is replaced by references to Revenue Business Income Manual BIM 61000–61075 (leasing: general) and BIM 61100–61195 (finance leasing).

71.69    **Legal and professional expenses.** In the second paragraph, the reference to the Revenue Inspector's Manual is replaced by a reference to Revenue Business Income Manual BIM 46420.

71.71    **Mines, quarries etc.** The fourth paragraph is replaced with the following.

'For the Revenue's view of the treatment of payments by mining concerns to landowners for restoration for surface damage, see Revenue Business Income Manual BIM 62025. In particular, a payment of compensation for ascertained past damage is allowable, as is a provision for such expenditure where made in accordance with generally accepted accounting practice and accurately quantified.'

71.72    **Miscellaneous expenses and receipts.** In the paragraph headed 'Carers' (page 898), the reference to the Revenue Inspector's Manual is replaced by a reference to Revenue Business Income Manual BIM 52780–52800.

On page 899, at the end of the text on computer software, the reference to the Revenue Inspector's Manual is replaced by a reference to Revenue Business Income Manual BIM 35800–35865.

On page 900, at the end of the text on video tape rental, the reference to the Revenue Inspector's Manual is replaced by a reference to Revenue Business Income Manual BIM 67200–67220.

The following paragraph is then added.

'**Websites.** The cost of setting up a website is likely to be capital expenditure; the regular update costs are likely to be revenue expenses (see Revenue Business Income Manual BIM 35870).'

71.74    **Personal expenses.** The final paragraph is replaced with the following two paragraphs.

'The personal costs (e.g. accommodation, food and drink) of a UK resident individual chargeable under Schedule D, Case I or Case II of living abroad on business are not disallowed under *ICTA 1988, s 74(1)(a)* or *(b)* (Revenue Business Income Manual BIM 47710 and Revenue Pamphlet IR 131, A16).

For the 'dual purpose rule' in relation to expenditure with an intrinsic duality of purpose, e.g. food, warmth, health and shelter, see Revenue Business Income Manual BIM 37900–37970.'

71.77    **Property sales and other property receipts.** In the first paragraph, the reference to the Revenue Inspector's Manual is replaced by a reference to Revenue Business Income Manual BIM 51500–51665. In the last full paragraph on page 902, reference to the Inspector's Manual is replaced by a reference to Business Income Manual BIM 51555.

71.78    **Rents etc. for business premises.** On page 906, under the heading 'Reverse premiums', the reference to the Revenue Inspector's Manual is replaced by a reference to Revenue Business Income Manual BIM 41050–41145.

71.79    **Repairs and renewals.** In sub-paragraph *(a)* (General), the reference to the Revenue Inspector's Manual is replaced by a reference to Revenue Business Income Manual BIM 46515, 46901.

In the second paragraph of sub-paragraph (*b*) (Business premises), the reference to the Inspector's Manual is replaced by a reference to Business Income Manual BIM 46901. At the end of that paragraph (on page 907), the following sentence is added.

'It should be noted that the Revenue view is that *Jenners* would have been decided differently if FRS 12 had been in operation at the time (see Revenue Business Income Manual BIM 46550).'

Towards the end of sub-paragraph (*b*), the reference to the Inspector's Manual is replaced by a reference to Business Income Manual BIM 46906.

A new sub-paragraph (*d*) is added as follows.

'**Assets held under an operating lease.** A deduction may be allowed for a provision to cover future repairs of assets held under an operating lease which contains a repairing obligation (for example, tenants' repairing leases of property). The obligation, required under FRS 12 (see (*b*) above), subsists from the signing of the lease. (Revenue Business Income Manual BIM 46535). It is unlikely the Revenue would have accepted such a deduction prior to the decision in *Jenners* at (*b*) above.'

At the end of 71.79, the reference to the Inspector's Manual is replaced by a reference to Business Income Manual BIM 46900–46970.

71.80    **Scientific research and research and development.** The full text is replaced with the following.

'Revenue expenditure incurred by a trader on 'research and development' (previously, for 1999/2000 and earlier years, on scientific research) related to his trade, whether undertaken directly or on his behalf, is allowable as a deduction from profits. Expenditure incurred in the acquisition of rights in, or arising out of, the research and development is excluded, but the allowable expenditure otherwise includes all expenditure incurred in, or providing facilities for, carrying it out. Research and development 'related' to a trade includes any which may lead to or facilitate an extension of the trade, or which is of a medical nature and has a special relation to the welfare of workers employed in the trade. These provisions apply equally to expenditure on oil and gas exploration and appraisal (within *ICTA 1988, s 837B*). [*ICTA 1988, s 82A; CAA 1990, ss 136, 139(1)(3); FA 2000, s 68, Sch 19 para 5*].

Relief is similarly given for any sum paid to a scientific research association having as its object scientific research related (with the extended meaning referred to above) to the class of trade concerned, or to any approved university etc., for such research. The association or university must be approved by the Secretary of State. '*Scientific research*' means any activities in the fields of natural or applied science for the extension of knowledge. Any question as to what constitutes scientific research is to be referred by the Board to the Secretary of State, whose decision is final. [*ICTA 1988, s 82B; CAA 1990, ss 136, 139(1)(3); FA 2000, Sch 19 para 5*].

It should be noted that these reliefs are given to trades and *not* to professions or vocations.

For *capital* outlay, see 10.52 CAPITAL ALLOWANCES.

'*Research and development*' means activities that fall to be treated as such in accordance with generally accepted accounting practice (see 71.40 above). However, this is subject to Treasury regulations which narrow the definition by reference to guidelines issued by the Department of Trade and Industry (DTI). [*ICTA 1988, s 837A; FA 2000, Sch 19 para 1*]. The latest regulations have effect for 2004/05 onwards and refer to DTI guidelines issued on 5 March 2004 (for which see www.dti.gov.uk/support/rd-guidelines-2004.htm). [*SI 2004 No 712*]. The previous regulations referred to guidelines issued on 28 July 2000 (see www.dti.gov.uk/support/rndguide.htm) which are revoked from 2004/05 onwards. [*SI 2000 No 2081*].

For enhanced tax reliefs for research and development expenditure by *companies*, see Tolley's Corporation Tax under Profit Computations.'

71.83   **Stock in trade and work in progress.** In line 1, the reference to the Revenue Inspector's Manual is replaced by a reference to Revenue Business Income Manual BIM 33000–33630.

The first sentence of the second paragraph is replaced with 'The general rule has long been that stock is to be valued at the lower of cost and market value.'.

The third paragraph is replaced with the following.

'However, the Revenue now take the view that any valuation of stock included in financial statements prepared in accordance with generally accepted accounting practice (see 71.40 above) should be accepted provided that

• it reflects the correct application of the principles of normal accountancy,

• the method pays sufficient regard to the facts, and

• the basis does not violate the taxing statutes as interpreted by the courts.

(Revenue Business Income Manual BIM 33115).

A mark to market basis of valuation, used mainly by financial institutions and commodity dealers and under which stock is valued at market value, may also be acceptable (Revenue Business Income Manual BIM 33160).

The principal accounting standard governing stock is SSAP 9.'

At the end of the text immediately preceding the heading 'Changes in basis of valuation' (foot of page 913), the following is added.

'It has been suggested that an amendment by the Accounting Standards Board to FRS 5 'Reporting the Substance of Transactions' requires professional work in progress to be valued at *selling price* beginning with accounts ended on after 23 December 2003 (Taxation Vol 152, No 3941 p 376, 22 January 2004); however, not all commentators interpret the amendment in this way (Taxation Vol 152, No 3944 p 447, 12 February 2004).'

The first full paragraph on page 914 is replaced with the following.

'Where there is a change in the basis of valuation, the following practice is applied for tax purposes. If the bases of valuation both before and after the change are valid bases, the opening figure for the period of change must be the same as the closing figure for the preceding period. If the change is from an invalid basis to a valid one, the opening figure for the period of change must be arrived at on the same basis as the closing figure for that period, and liabilities for earlier years will be reviewed where it is possible to do so. (Revenue Pamphlet IR 131, SP 3/90, 10 January 1990 and see now Revenue Business Income Manual BIM 33199). See, however, *Woodall-Duckham Ltd* (above) as regards long-term contracts.'

The immediately following reference to the Revenue Inspector's Manual is deleted.

In the paragraph headed 'Long-term contracts', a reference is added to Revenue Business Income Manual BIM 33025.

In the paragraph headed 'Goods sold subject to reservation of title', the reference to the Inspector's Manual is replaced by a reference to Business Income Manual BIM 33375.

In the penultimate paragraph on page 916, the reference to the Inspector's Manual is replaced by a reference to Business Income Manual BIM 33520.

71.85   **Subsidies, grants etc.** The opening paragraph is replaced with the following.

'Payments under the **Business Start up scheme**, to assist unemployed people in setting up their own businesses, are made under *Employment and Training Act 1973, s 2(2)(d) or*

*Enterprise and New Towns (Scotland) Act 1990, s 2(4)(c)* (or NI equivalent). They are chargeable to tax under Schedule D, Case VI rather than Case I. This treatment does not, however, prevent the payments being treated as earned income or as 'relevant earnings' for personal pension scheme and retirement annuity purposes (see 59.8 PERSONAL PENSION SCHEMES, 65.7 RETIREMENT ANNUITIES). They may also continue to give rise to liability to Class 4 national insurance contributions. [*ICTA 1988, s 127, Sch 29 para 14*]. The payments are made by Training and Enterprise Councils (in Scotland, Local Enterprise Councils). The legislation refers to payments of *Enterprise Allowance* (which preceded the Business Start up scheme), but applies equally to payments under the current scheme provided they retain the essential characteristics of Enterprise Allowance, in particular that the applicant is unemployed or working notice and that the allowance is a flat rate weekly amount. (Lump sum payments are outside the scope of the above and are likely to be taxable as Case I trading receipts.) Where the business is run through a company, the payments are made to the individual as agent of the company and are treated as Case VI income of the company. (Revenue Business Income Manual BIM 40400, 40405).'

In the paragraph headed 'Fishing grants', the reference to the Revenue Inspector's Manual is replaced by a reference to Revenue Business Income Manual BIM 57001.

In the paragraph headed 'Research grant' at the top of page 919, the reference to the Inspector's Manual is replaced by a reference to Business Income Manual BIM 65151.

71.87    **Telecommunications licences.** The final paragraph is replaced with the following.

'For articles giving the Revenue's view on the interpretation of *FA 2000, Sch 23*, see Revenue Tax Bulletins December 2000 pp 815–817, February 2004 p 1094. For corporation tax purposes, *FA 2000, Sch 23* is superseded for accounting periods ending on or after 1 April 2002 by *FA 2002, Sch 29* (see Tolley's Corporation Tax under Intangible Assets).'

71.88    **Tied petrol stations etc.** In the third paragraph, the case of *McClymont and Another v Jarman (Sp C 387) 2003, [2004] SSCD 54* is added to the initial list of citations (exclusivity payments held to be capital receipts).

71.89    **Training.** In the second paragraph, the reference to the Revenue Inspector's Manual is replaced by a reference to Revenue Business Income Manual BIM 47651.

71.90    **Travelling and subsistence expenses.** In the paragraph headed 'Motoring expenses' at the foot of page 921, the reference to the Revenue Inspector's Manual is replaced by a reference to Revenue Business Income Manual BIM 47701.

At the end (on page 922), the following paragraph is added.

'For car hire, see 71.68 above. For travelling and subsistence generally, see Revenue Business Income Manual BIM 47700–47710. For the 'dual purpose rule' in relation to travel and subsistence costs, see BIM 37600–37630, 37660.'

71.93    **Value added tax.** In the final paragraph, the reference to the Revenue Inspector's Manual is replaced by a reference to Revenue Business Income Manual BIM 31500–31625.

71.94    **Waste disposal.** Two-thirds of the way down page 925, the reference to the Revenue Inspector's Manual is replaced by a reference to Revenue Business Income Manual BIM 67405–67520.

# 72    Schedule D, Case III

72.2    **Relevant discounted securities.** At the end of paragraph spanning pages 933 and 934, the following is added.

'For disposals of strips after 14 January 2004, where there is a scheme or arrangement to obtain a tax advantage, market value (computed solely by reference to publicly available pricing information) will be substituted for acquisition cost and disposal proceeds, thus limiting the allowable loss to the loss (if any) sustained by reference to any decrease in market value between acquisition and disposal. Furthermore, a loss on an actual or deemed disposal (other than as part of a scheme or arrangement) of a strip acquired after 14 January 2004 will be disallowed to the extent that proceeds fall below acquisition cost. The legislation will be in *FA 2004*. (Revenue Press Release 15 January 2004).' See also the Budget Summary.

# 75    Schedule E—Employment Income

The Revenue Schedule E Manual referred to throughout this chapter is now called the Revenue Employment Income Manual, but paragraph numbers therein are generally unchanged.

75.4    **Employee resident, ordinarily resident or domiciled outside the UK.** The fourth paragraph is amended to substitute earnings within *ITEPA 2003, s 25* and *s 26* for emoluments chargeable under Schedule E, Case II or III, but the thrust of SP 5/84 is unchanged.

75.10    **General earnings.** The fourth full paragraph on page 976 ('money's worth') is replaced with the following.

'Whether 'money's worth' received by an employee comes to him as an emolument may be a difficult question of fact. For modern examples see *Hochstrasser v Mayes HL 1959, 38 TC 673* (compensation for loss on sale of house on transfer, held not assessable); *Wilcock v Eve Ch D 1995, 67 TC 223* (payment for loss of rights under share option scheme, held not assessable), and contrast *Hamblett v Godfrey CA 1986, 59 TC 694* (payment for loss of trade union etc. rights, held assessable); *Laidler v Perry HL 1965, 42 TC 351*; *Brumby v Milner HL 1976, 51 TC 583*; *Tyrer v Smart HL 1978, 52 TC 533*. The meeting by the employer of a **pecuniary liability** of the employee constitutes money's worth, see e.g. *Hartland v Diggines HL 1926, 10 TC 247* (tax liability), *Nicoll v Austin KB 1935, 19 TC 531* (rates etc. of employee's residence), and *Glynn v CIR PC 1990, 63 TC 162* (payment direct to school of child's school fees); this applies to payment of the employee's council tax (Revenue Press Release 16 March 1993), and may apply to payment of employees' parking fines. In the latter case, the tax treatment depends on whether the vehicle is owned by employer or by employee and whether the fixed penalty notice is affixed to the car or handed to the driver (see Revenue Employment Income Manual EIM 21686 for a full summary). Congestion charges paid by an employer in connection with an employee-owned vehicle are taxable (see Revenue Employment Income Manual EIM 21680). For specific items and legislation modifying the general rule, see 75.12 onwards below.'

In the second paragraph on page 977 (homeworker employees), the text following the statutory reference is replaced with the following.

'Up to £2 per week can be paid without the need to justify the amount paid or to provide supporting evidence of the expenses incurred; for larger payments, the employer must be able to provide supporting evidence that the payment falls wholly within the above exemption (Revenue Press Release REV BN 3, 9 April 2003). See also Revenue Employment Income Manual EIM 01472–01478 and Revenue Tax Bulletin December 2003 pp 1068, 1069.'

75.11    **Allowable deductions.** At the top of page 981, the following paragraph is added.

'Rental of *second* telephone line at employee's home allowed where used exclusively for business calls and there is a genuine business need for the line (but rental of first line or single line not allowed) (Revenue Employment Income Manual EIM 32940).'

# 75    Schedule E—Employment Income

At the end of sub-paragraph (*b*) on page 981, the following paragraph is added.

'No deduction permitted for broadband internet access where employee is able to use the internet for non-business purposes (Revenue Employment Income Manual EIM 32940).'

75.16    **Benefits-in-kind generally.** Immediately before the final paragraph of sub-paragraph (i) (see page 986), the following paragraph is added.

'The exemption can extend to the provision of a telephone line and/or broadband internet access in the employee's home (Revenue Employment Income Manual EIM 21615, 21616). See generally EIM 21610–21615.'

At the end of sub-paragraph (xvii) (exemption for childcare facilities) on page 988, the following paragraph is added.

'The exemption is to be extended from 6 April 2005 to childcare away from the workplace. Employers will be able to either contract directly with a nursery, childminder or after-school club on behalf of employees or provide childcare vouchers to employees; in each case, the benefit will be tax-free up to a maximum of £50 per week. The childcare used must be registered childcare or approved home-childcare, and the scheme must be generally accessible to all staff. (Revenue Press Release 10 December 2003).'

In sub-paragraph (xxiii) (exemption for mobile telephones) (see page 989) the following is added (for clarification).

'The exemption covers the telephone itself, any line rental and any calls, business or private, paid for by the employer on that telephone (Revenue Employment Income Manual EIM 21780).'

At the end of sub-paragraph (xxiv) (exemption for computer equipment) (see page 989), the following is added.

'For the interaction between this exemption and *ITEPA 2003, s 206* (cost of benefit on subsequent transfer of asset), see Revenue Employment Income Manual EIM 21652.'

75.18    **Motor vehicles provided for private use.** Immediately before the first full paragraph on page 994, the following paragraph is added.

'The special basis of charge does *not* apply where the car is in the *co-ownership* of the employer and employee (the cash equivalent of the benefit for tax purposes being instead computed as in 75.16 above by reference to the employer's interest in the car) (*Vasili v Christensen (Sp C 377), [2003] SSCD 428*).'

In the paragraph on page 994 beginning 'Where such a special basis of charge applies ...', the text preceding the statutory references is replaced with the following.

'Where such a special basis of charge applies, no other charge arises in respect of any expenses or reimbursements etc. in relation to the vehicle or in respect of vouchers for their provision (e.g. insurance, road tax, congestion charges). It appears that this does not apply to the payment of fines by the employer (although parking fines may escape liability in certain circumstances — see Revenue Employment Income Manual EIM 21686). The provision of a driver is a separate benefit under 75.16 above (subject to an expense claim for business use).'

At the top of page 1006, at the end of sub-paragraph (iv) (Fuel for private use: 2002/03 and earlier years), the following paragraph is added.

'Providing that all the miles of private travel have been properly identified, the Revenue will accept that there is no fuel charge where the employer uses the appropriate advisory rate from the table in (v) below, first published in January 2002, to work out the cost of fuel used for private travel that the employee must make good (Revenue Employment Income Manual EIM 23781). See (v) below for further detail.'

At the foot of page 1006, in sub-paragraph (v) (Fuel for private use: 2003/04 and subsequent years), the following is added.

'Providing that all the miles of private travel have been properly identified, the Revenue will accept that there is no fuel charge where the employer uses the appropriate rate from the table below (or any higher rate) to work out the cost of fuel used for private travel that the employee must make good. These advisory rates are not binding where the employer can demonstrate that employees cover the full cost of private fuel by repaying at a lower rate per mile. Even if it seems that the actual cost of the fuel could be more than, for example, 14p a mile for a 2.5 litre petrol car, it is only in exceptional cases that they will argue that a higher repayment rate should apply; they will always accept the use of the advisory rates where the engine size is 3 litres or less.

| *Engine size* | *Petrol* | *Diesel* | *LPG\** |
|---|---|---|---|
| 1400 cc or less | 10p | 9p | 6p |
| 1401 cc to 2000cc | 12p | 9p | 7p |
| Over 2000 cc | 14p | 12p | 9p |

\* LPG = Liquid Petroleum Gas

(Revenue Employment Income Manual EIM 23781).'

75.20   **Cheap loan arrangements.** It is noted that the 'official rate' has been determined in advance for 2004/05 at 5% (unchanged from 2003/04). See Revenue Press Release 12 January 2004.

75.27   **Employment or profession?** In the paragraph headed 'Artistes' on page 1022, the reference to the Revenue Inspector's Manual is replaced by a reference to Revenue Business Income Manual BIM 50151.

75.32   **Living accommodation etc.** The paragraph at the top of page 1030 is replaced with the following.

"Living accommodation' for these purposes includes all kinds of residential accommodation - e.g. mansions, houses, flats, houseboats, holiday homes or apartments - but not overnight or hotel accommodation or board and lodging (Revenue Employment Income Manual EIM 11321). Whether such accommodation is provided for an employee is a question of fact — see Revenue Employment Income Manual EIM 11405, 11406.'

75.37   **Restrictive covenants.** At the end, the following paragraph is added.

'Where a compromise agreement made at termination of employment includes a repayment clause (typically a clause requiring full or partial repayment by the employee of the sum settled if he subsequently initiates litigation in respect of the employment or its termination), the attribution of any of the sum settled to the undertaking not to litigate would be outside SP 3/96 and thus within the above charging provisions. Other than in exceptional cases, e.g. where the sum settled is clearly excessive in the circumstances, the Revenue will not seek to make such an attribution and a charge under the above provisions will not arise. It should be noted that if, exceptionally, a charge *does* arise, there can be no subsequent adjustment to the charge if a repayment is, in fact, made under the clause. (Revenue Tax Bulletin October 2003 p 1063).'

75.39   **Shares etc.** In the fourth paragraph, the reference to the Revenue Inspector's Manual is replaced by a reference to Revenue Share Schemes Manual SSM 4.4.

At the end, the following paragraph is added.

'*Phantom share schemes.* Some employers may set up incentive schemes involving 'phantom' or hypothetical shares; the employee is 'allocated' a number of shares in the employer company and potentially receives a future cash bonus linked to the value of those shares. No tax is chargeable at the time of the award (as no value passes), the bonus being chargeable as general earnings for, usually but not invariably, the tax year of receipt. After 15 April 2003, an employee's rights under a phantom share scheme are a 'security' for the purposes of the employee shares legislation (being rights under a contract for differences or similar contract — see 82.3 SHARE-RELATED EMPLOYMENT INCOME AND EXEMPTIONS); consequently the bonus may alternatively be taxed as a post-acquisition benefit from securities (see 82.12 SHARE-RELATED EMPLOYMENT INCOME AND EXEMPTIONS). (Revenue Employment Income Manual EIM 01600).'

75.46    **Travelling, subsistence etc.** In the paragraph headed 'Travelling appointments' on page 1056, the last sentence is replaced with the following.

'The Revenue has agreed a tax-free overnight subsistence allowance of £25.15 (from 1 January 2003 – £24.50 for calendar year 2002, £24.30 for 2001, £23.55 for 2000, £23.22 for 1999, £22.55 for 1998, £21.75 for 1997, £21.15 for 1996) (reduced by 25% where a sleeper cab is available) under certain industry agreements.'

# 78    Self-Assessment

78.1    **Introduction.** In the second paragraph, it is noted that Revenue booklet SAT 2 was replaced in October 2003 by a Revenue Manual, 'Income Tax Self-Assessment: The Legal Framework'. Immediately above the heading 'Payment of tax' on page 1069, the following paragraph is added.

'A four-page Short Tax Return (STR) for those with relatively simple tax affairs is being piloted and is expected to be rolled out nationwide in April 2005. Under new criteria applicable from April 2004, fewer taxpayers (including higher rate taxpayers) whose affairs can be adequately dealt with using the PAYE system will be asked to complete a tax return of any kind, though they may choose to do so if they wish. From April 2004, the Revenue will make increased use of the telephone to resolve minor queries arising in connection with completed returns. (Revenue Tax Bulletin February 2004 pp 1079, 1080).'

78.3    **Self-assessments.** In the final paragraph, the reference to Revenue booklet SAT 2 is replaced by a reference to Revenue Income Tax Self-Assessment: The Legal Framework Manual SALF 204, para 2.33.

# 81    Settlements

81.1    **Introduction.** The following paragraph is added.

'It was announced in the December 2003 Pre-Budget Report that the Government are to consult on a new and modernised income tax and capital gains tax regime for trusts, to be implemented from 6 April 2005. Details of the proposals are on the Revenue's website.' See also the Budget Summary.

81.5    **Discretionary and accumulation trusts.** At the end of sub-paragraph (iv) on page 1086, the following is added.

'(See also *Red Discretionary Trustees v Inspector of Taxes (Sp C 397) 2003, 2004 STI 314* as regards the application of the Schedule F trust rate to stock dividends.)'

Then, immediately after sub-paragraphs (i)–(v), the following paragraph is added.

'The rate applicable to trusts and the Schedule F trust rate are expected to increase to 40% and 32½% respectively for 2004/05 onwards (Pre-Budget Report, December 2003).' See also the Budget Summary.

81.16    **Definitions etc.** In sub-paragraph (*a*), immediately before the penultimate paragraph on page 1094, the following two paragraphs are added.

'A detailed joint response by seven professional bodies, including CIOT and ICAEW, was published on 11 September 2003 (and reproduced at *2003 STI 1605* and at www.tax.org.uk/ attach.pl/1932/753/s660A%20paper%20final100903.doc). This reflects the bodies' concerns both as to the Revenue's interpretation of the settlements legislation as summarised above and as to its retrospective nature and makes clear that they do not accept a number of key technical issues that underpin the above guidance.

The Revenue responded with an article in their February 2004 Tax Bulletin. It contains no relaxation of their views. The examples included in the original article are revisited purely for the purpose of setting out the entries required on self-assessment tax returns where the settlements legislation applies. A number of new examples are also included. (Revenue Tax Bulletin February 2004 pp 1085–1094).'

# 82    Share-Related Employment Income and Exemptions

82.2    **General.** At the end of the ante-penultimate paragraph (self-assessment implications), the following is added.

'See Revenue Share Focus Newsletter December 2003 pp 1, 2 for new Revenue procedures for dealing with late filing of returns by employers and by others with reporting obligations.'

The final paragraph is replaced with the following paragraphs.

'*Armed Forces Reservists.* By concession, backdated to 7 January 2003 (the date of the first call-up order for service in Iraq), a reservist called up for service under *Reserve Forces Act 1996* will have his consequent employment with the Ministry of Defence (MOD) treated as fulfilling the employment conditions for the approved schemes at 82.20, 82.47 and 82.61 below and for enterprise management incentives at 82.35 below. In addition, employers and scheme providers may take such action as is necessary to maintain the reservist's participation in the scheme for the period they are away serving with the MOD; provided the action does no more than that, it will not compromise the approval of the scheme. (Revenue Extra-Statutory Concession A103, 16 July 2003). Guidance notes for employers, setting out possible courses of action within the concession, are attached to the published concession.

*Earn-outs.* Where the consideration passing on the sale of a business includes an earn-out, typically a right to receive securities in the purchasing company after a certain period of time has elapsed and dependent on the performance of the newly taken-over business, any element of remuneration for services as an employee or prospective employee included in the earn-out may give rise to a tax charge under the provisions at 82.4 below (restricted shares), 82.6 below (convertible shares) or 82.16 below (unapproved share options) as it has effect after *FA 2003*, whichever is relevant, always bearing in mind the extended meaning of 'shares' at 82.3 below. Guidance has been issued as to how the rules will be applied and how to identify if an earn-out is 'remuneration' or further sale consideration or an element of both. See www.inlandrevenue.gov.uk/shareschemes/faq_emprelatedsecurity-ch5.htm#1

Two *Memoranda of Understanding* between the Revenue and the British Venture Capital Association, covering certain matters arising from the substantial changes made by *FA 2003* to the provisions at 82.3–82.17 below, were published on 25 July 2003 and are available at the Revenue's website.'

82.4    **Restricted shares.** It is noted that the appointed day was 1 September 2003 as expected — by virtue of *SI 2003 No 1997* — and that prescribed forms of election under these provisions were published on the Revenue's website on 22 July 2003 and 6 October 2003 (the latter being specially for use where the restricted shares are acquired on exercise of a qualifying enterprise management incentives option).

The second full paragraph on page 1109 is replaced with the following.

'Either election could also be made, with appropriate modifications, in relation to shares acquired after 15 April 2003 but before 1 September 2003. In this case, the deadline for implementing the election was 15 September 2003. Such an election could not, however, be made if, in relation to the shares, a tax charge arose under 82.5 or 82.14(*a*) below.'

82.8    **Anti-avoidance — shares with artificially depressed market value.** The first full paragraph on page 1118 is replaced with the following.

'If, however, the tax exemption on acquisition at 82.4 above applied in relation to the shares, the period taken into account for the purpose of both the above charges (normally a seven-year period) is extended back to a point seven years before the acquisition of the shares.'

82.13    **Post-acquisition benefits from shares before FA 2003.** In the last complete paragraph on page 1123, the reference to the Revenue Inspector's Manual is replaced by a reference to Revenue Share Schemes Manual SSM 4.4. An identical change is made in the third paragraph of 82.14.

82.16    **Unapproved share options.** In the penultimate paragraph on page 1130, the reference to the Revenue Inspector's Manual is replaced by a reference to Revenue Share Schemes Manual SSM 4.4.

Immediately before the last paragraph on that page, the following paragraph is added.

'A gain realised following cessation of the employment on the exercise, assignment, release etc. of an employment-related share option falls within *these* provisions and not those at 19 COMPENSATION FOR LOSS OF EMPLOYMENT (AND DAMAGES) (*Bluck v Salton (Sp C 378), [2003] SSCD 439*).'

82.23    **Partnership shares.** In the first complete paragraph on page 1144, the first sentence is replaced with the following two sentences.

'Subject to the above, for these purposes an employee's salary means his earnings (from the employment in question) otherwise subject to PAYE, excluding any taxable benefits and expenses within 75.16–75.24 SCHEDULE E—EMPLOYMENT INCOME. The Revenue take this to mean salary after deduction of allowable pension contributions and charitable donations made under payroll giving schemes (Revenue Share Focus Newsletter December 2003 p 8).'

82.37    **Income tax consequences of qualifying option.** Immediately before the final paragraph on page 1158, the following paragraph is added.

'For guidance on the interaction between the above rules and the restricted shares rules at 82.4 above (where the shares acquired on exercise are restricted shares), see www.inlandrevenue.gov.uk/shareschemes/faq_emprelatedsecurity-ch2.htm#w'

82.39    **Qualifying trades.** In the first full paragraph on page 1163, the cross-reference to 10.52 CAPITAL ALLOWANCES is replaced with a cross-reference to 71.80 SCHEDULE D, CASES I AND II and it is noted that the latest DTI guidelines issued on 5 March 2004 have no effect in relation to EMI share options granted before 6 April 2004.

82.42    **Replacement options.** In the final paragraph (page 1166), the first sentence is replaced with the following.

'For the purposes of the enterprise management incentives provisions, a replacement option which is a qualifying option is treated as if granted on the date the original option was granted. (This does not apply for the purposes of the 'notice of grant' provisions at 82.43 below — Revenue Share Focus Newsletter December 2003 pp 8, 9.)'

82.67   **Limit on value of shares subject to options.** At the end, the following is added.

'Where an option is granted that causes the £30,000 limit to be exceeded, the whole of that option (and not just the excess) becomes an unapproved share option (Revenue Share Focus Newsletter December 2003 p 3).'

# 83   Social Security

83.5   **Benefits under Government pilot schemes.** At the end, the following is added.

'A further Order exempts from 1 October 2003 payments made under the two schemes known as the Employment Retention and Advancement Scheme and the Return to Work Credit Scheme. [*SI 2003 No 2339*]. A further Order exempts from 6 April 2004 payments made under the two schemes known as Working Neighbourhoods Pilot and In-Work Credit. [*SI 2004 No 575*].'

83.7   **Child tax credit and working tax credit.** The 2004/05 figures, taken from the December 2003 Pre-Budget Report, are added.

83.8   **National insurance contributions.** See Budget Summary for rates/amounts of contributions due for 2004/05.

# 89   Underwriters at Lloyd's

89.6   **Losses.** The final paragraph is replaced with the following.

'An *anticipated* underwriting loss may not be taken into account in a PAYE coding until title to it has been established, i.e. until it has actually been sustained (*Blackburn v Keeling CA, [2003] STC 1162*). Whilst awaiting this decision of the CA, which reversed an earlier Ch D decision, the Revenue were prepared to take account of provisional 2001 underwriting losses (i.e. 2004/05 losses) in 2003/04 PAYE codes if requested to do so, i.e. on the assumption that the loss would be carried back (Lloyd's Market Bulletin 28 May 2003).'

# 90   Unit Trusts

90.1   **Authorised unit trusts.** The first full paragraph on page 1217 is extended as follows.

'The Revenue have wide-ranging powers to make provision by regulations to give effect to the deduction provisions. See *SI 2003 No 1830* which modifies the deduction provisions in relation to interest distributions made to or received under a trust and also provides the Revenue with general powers to obtain information from trustees of unit trusts, and inspect their records, for the purpose of determining whether interest distributions made gross were properly so made. In the case of distributions made to or received under a trust, the residence condition requirement is for a valid declaration from the trustees both that they are non-UK resident and that each beneficiary known to them is non-UK ordinarily resident or, in the case of a corporate beneficiary, non-UK resident. If, however, the whole of the distribution is, or falls to be treated as, income of a person other than the trustees, the normal provisions apply as if that person were the unit holder.'

## 91   Venture Capital Trusts

At the end, the following paragraph is added.

'Subject to appropriate modifications (see *SI 1997 No 1154* as amended), the tax legislation relating to authorised unit trusts has effect in like manner in relation to open-ended investment companies.'

## 91   Venture Capital Trusts

91.3   **Qualifying holdings.** In the paragraph on page 1224 beginning 'The definition of 'controlling interest' ...' , the cross-reference to 10.52 CAPITAL ALLOWANCES is replaced with a cross-reference to 71.80 SCHEDULE D, CASES I AND II and it is noted that the latest DTI guidelines issued on 5 March 2004 have no effect for these purposes in relation to shares or securities issued before 6 April 2004.

91.5   **Relief in respect of investments.** At the end of the first paragraph, it is noted that the December 2003 Pre-Budget Report included a proposal to increase the £100,000 limit to £200,000 from 6 April 2004. See also the Budget Summary.

# Budget Summary 17 March 2004

**Note:** *It must be remembered that these proposals are subject to amendment during the passage of the Finance Bill.*

| PERSONAL TAXATION | 2004/05 | 2003/04 |
|---|---|---|
| *Personal allowance* | | |
| general | £4,745 | £4,615 |
| aged 65 or over in year | | |
| of assessment | £6,830 | £6,610 |
| aged 75 or over in year | | |
| of assessment | £6,950 | £6,720 |
| age allowance income limit | £18,900 | £18,300 |
| minimum where income | | |
| exceeds limit | £4,745 | £4,615 |
| *Married couple's allowance* | | |
| (10% relief) | | |
| either spouse born before | | |
| 6 April 1935 | £5,725 | £5,565 |
| either spouse aged 75 or | | |
| over in year of | | |
| assessment | £5,795 | £5,635 |
| age allowance income limit | £18,900 | £18,300 |
| minimum where income | | |
| exceeds limit | £2,210 | £2,150 |
| *Blind person's allowance* | £1,560 | £1,510 |
| *Income tax rates* | | |
| Starting rate | 10% | 10% |
| on taxable income up to | £2,020 | £1,960 |
| Basic rate | 22% | 22% |
| on taxable income from | | |
| starting rate limit up to | £31,400 | £30,500 |
| Higher rate | 40% | 40% |
| on taxable income over | £31,400 | £30,500 |
| Lower rate | | |
| on certain interest income | 20% | 20% |
| Lower rate | | |
| on dividend income | 10% | 10% |
| Higher rate | | |
| on dividend income | 32.5% | 32.5% |

| COMPANY TAXATION | FY2004 | FY2003 |
|---|---|---|
| *Corporation tax rates* | | |
| All companies (except below) | 30% | 30% |
| Companies with small profits | 19% | 19% |
| — 19% rate limit | £300,000 | £300,000 |
| — marginal relief limit | £1,500,000 | £1,500,000 |
| — marginal rate | 32.75% | 32.75% |
| Starting rate | 0% | 0% |
| — 0% rate limit | £10,000 | £10,000 |
| — marginal relief limit | £50,000 | £50,000 |
| — marginal rate | 23.75% | 23.75% |
| Small company distributed profits | | |
| — minimum rate | 19% | — |

| CAPITAL GAINS TAX | 2004/05 | 2003/04 |
|---|---|---|
| Rate—general | 10%*:20%* :40%* | 10%*:20%*:40%* |
| —trustees and personal | | |
| representatives | 40%* | 34%* |
| General exemption limit | £8,200 | £7,900 |

*subject to taper relief where available

| INHERITANCE TAX | Transfers after 5/4/2004 |
|---|---|
| Threshold | £263,000 |
| Death rate | 40% |

| VAT | |
|---|---|
| Standard rate | 17.5% |
| Registration threshold after 31 March 2004 | £58,000 |

(previously £56,000 after 9 April 2003)

**NATIONAL INSURANCE**     2004/05

(2003/04 in brackets where different)

**Class 1 Contributions**

*Not contracted out*

The employee contribution is 11% of earnings between £91 (£89) and £610 (£595) p.w. plus 1% of all earnings above £610 (£595) p.w. The employer contribution is 12.8% of all earnings in excess of the first £91 (£89) p.w.

*Contracted out*

The 'not contracted out' rates for employees are reduced on the band of earnings from £91 (£89) p.w. to £610 (£595) p.w. by 1.6%. For employers, they are reduced on the band of earnings from £91 (£89) p.w. to £610 (£595) p.w. by 3.5% for employees in salary-related schemes or 1.0% for employees in money purchase schemes. In addition, there is an employee rebate of 1.6% and an employer rebate of 3.5% or 1.0%, as appropriate, on earnings from £79 (£77) p.w. up to £91 (£89) p.w.

| Class 1A and 1B contributions | | 12.8% |
|---|---|---|
| **Class 2 contributions** | | |
| Flat weekly rate | £2.05 | (£2.00) |
| Exemption limit | £4,215 | (£4,095) |
| **Class 3 contributions** | | |
| Flat weekly rate | £7.15 | (£6.95) |

**Class 4 contributions**

8% on the band of profits between £4,745 (£4,615) and £31,720 (£30,940) *plus* 1% on all profits above £31,720 (£30,940).

# Budget Summary

## Personal Taxation

### Income Tax Rates and Allowances

For 2004/05, the lower, basic and higher rates of income tax remain at 10%, 22% and 40% respectively. The starting rate band is increased by £60 to £2,020, and the basic rate band by £840 to £29,380 (so that the higher rate applies to taxable income in excess of £31,400).

The special rates applicable to dividends and other savings income are unchanged.

The income tax rates applicable to discretionary and accumulation trusts are increased to 32.5% (previously 25%) on dividend income and 40% (previously 34%) on other types of income.

The basic personal allowance is increased by £130 to £4,745. For this and other personal reliefs, see the table on the front page.

### Pension Schemes Earnings Cap

From 6 April 2004, the maximum level of earnings for which pension provision may be made under tax-approved occupational, personal pension and stakeholder pension schemes is increased by £3,000 to £102,000.

### New Simplified Self-Assessment Tax Return

From April 2004 over 400,000 taxpayers will be sent a new simplified self-assessment tax return instead of the main return, increasing from 50,000 in last year's pilot. The new form is likely to be rolled out nationally in 2005 with around 1.5m taxpayers receiving the short return. It takes the form of a four-page short tax return. There is no requirement to calculate the tax on the form and taxpayers will be encouraged to file by 30 September in order that the Revenue may calculate their tax due by 31 January. If needed there is a two-page simple calculation to give people a rough idea of their tax liability.

The short tax return will be issued automatically based on the information in the previous year's return. Taxpayers must ensure they are eligible to complete the short return as their circumstances may have changed. The form is aimed at those with simple affairs such as non-director employees or self-employed individuals with a turnover of less than £15,000.

The Revenue will process these returns using an automated data capture facility.

Taxpayers can also choose to file the return online.

### Simplification of the Pension Regime

After much consultation the Chancellor announced that a simplified pension regime will replace the eight existing tax regimes with effect from 6 April 2006. The new regime will encompass a single lifetime fund limit set at £1.5m in 2006 and increasing to £1.6m in 2007, £1.65m in 2008, £1.75m in 2009 and £1.8m in 2010.

Individuals can take a tax-free lump sum of up to 25% of their qualifying fund value at the time of vesting. Funds in excess of the lifetime limit will be subject to a recovery charge on vesting of 25% of the excess if the excess is used to buy an annuity, or 55% if it is taken as a lump sum.

There will be an annual contributions limit set initially at £215,000 and increasing steadily each year to an expected £255,000 in 2010. Where total annual contributions exceed the annual allowance, the excess will be chargeable on the individual.

Tax relief will be given on all employer contributions to an individual's pension scheme, subject to the spreading of large contributions. Individuals can obtain tax relief on their own contributions up to 100% of their earnings (or £3,600 if higher) for any given year.

The minimum pension age will rise from 50 to 55 by 2010. Drawdown will still be permissible and pensions must generally be secured by the age of 75.

From 6 April 2006 it will no longer be necessary for a member to leave employment in order to access an employer's occupational scheme.

Transitional rules will exist to protect individuals who wish to preserve their pre-6 April 2006 position.

**Venture Capital Schemes**

The annual investment limit for income tax relief under the Enterprise Investment Scheme (EIS) is increased from £150,000 to £200,000 for shares issued after 5 April 2004. For shares issued after 16 March 2004, a rule change will enable investors *not* seeking EIS reliefs to subscribe for shares otherwise than wholly in cash without prejudicing reliefs available to EIS investors subscribing wholly in cash. Also for shares issued after 16 March 2004, the rules on loans will be relaxed so that a company may repay a loan made to it by an investor without necessarily jeopardising his entitlement to EIS income tax and capital gains deferral reliefs on a subsequent investment in the company. Currently, an EIS company is allowed to have subsidiaries, but they must be 75% subsidiaries; in relation to shares issued after 16 March 2004, 51% subsidiaries are allowed, although any company whose activities benefit from the EIS moneys raised must still be a 90% subsidiary, as must any property management subsidiary. Finally, the 'active company' rule is to be amended to make it easier for groups to arrange which company carries on, at any time, the activity for which money is raised under the EIS.

For investments in qualifying Venture Capital Trust (VCT) shares issued in 2004/05 and 2005/06 only, the rate of income tax relief will be increased from 20% to 40%. The annual investment limit is doubled to £200,000 for shares acquired after 5 April 2004. Capital gains deferral relief will no longer be available for gains reinvested in shares issued after 5 April 2004. The rules regarding subsidiaries and the 'active company' rule are to be amended in similar fashion as for the EIS (see above).

Some alterations are made to the Corporate Venturing Scheme (CVS) to bring the rules for that scheme further into line with those for the EIS and for VCTs.

**Income Tax Charge on 'Pre-Owned Assets'**

An income tax charge is to be imposed from 2005/06 onwards on the annual benefit of using or enjoying an asset that was once owned by the user (and has not been sold by him at an arm's length price for cash), where such use is enjoyed free of charge or at below market rent. The charge will also apply to assets which the user did not formerly own but which were purchased with funds provided by him. Both tangible and intangible assets will be within the charge. The rules will quantify an annual taxable value for the benefit – modelled on the existing rules for taxing benefits in kind provided to employees (but the precise details are still to be finalised), with relief given for any amount paid by the taxpayer for the benefit (eg rent). No income tax charge will apply where the total taxable value for any tax year is less than £2,500. If the asset in question still forms part of the taxpayer's estate for inheritance tax purposes, under the 'gifts with reservation' rules, the asset will not fall within the income tax charge. In addition, the charge will not apply where:

- the asset ceased to be owned before 18 March 1986; or
- the asset is now owned by the taxpayer's spouse; or
- the taxpayer was formerly owner of the asset only by virtue of a will or intestacy subsequently varied; or
- the use or enjoyment is merely incidental.

The charge applies to UK residents. For those not domiciled in the UK, the charge is restricted to their UK assets. For those becoming domiciled in the UK, the charge will not thereafter apply to any non-UK assets which they ceased to own before acquiring UK domicile.

Pre-existing arrangements will escape the new charge if they are dismantled, or the user begins paying full market rent, before the start date of 6 April 2005. Alternatively, a taxpayer may elect, by 31 January 2007, to remain outside the income tax charge (in relation to the asset(s) specified in the election), but in that case the asset in question will be treated as part of their estate for inheritance tax purposes while they continue to enjoy it.

**Jointly Owned Shares in Close Companies**

From 6 April 2004, income distributions from shares in a close company that are jointly owned by a married couple will no longer automatically be split 50/50, subject to an election for the split to be based on the actual proportion of ownership and entitlement to the income. Instead, the split along actual ownership lines will apply automatically.

# Budget Summary

### Immediate Needs Annuities

It is current practice to treat payments by insurance companies under annuity contracts to fund long-term care as not liable to tax. Some doubt has arisen over this treatment, so legislation is being introduced to confirm that it is correct. It will apply from 1 October 2004 to both existing and new policies.

New legislation will also ensure that the profits from writing such business are taxed according to the normal rules applying to trading profits from permanent health insurance business.

### Lloyd's Underwriters

Lloyd's Underwriters (Names) who transfer their underwriting to a company in which they are the majority shareholder, or to a Scottish Limited Partnership (SLP) in which they are the only underwriting partner, will be able to set off trading losses from underwriting years before the transfer against income derived from the company, or against partnership trading profits, from underwriting years after the transfer. Immediately before the transfer of the business, the Name must own over 50% of the company's ordinary share capital and also control it. Where the transfer is to an SLP of which he or she is the sole member carrying on underwriting business, income tax losses will be carried forward to set against the member's share of the partnership profits from the underwriting business.

Names may also be able to defer liability to capital gains tax (CGT) where their underwriting activities are taken over by a company and they transfer assets to the company in exchange for an issue of its shares. Chargeable gains arising (net of losses) on disposals of syndicate capacity and assets held as Funds at Lloyd's (FAL) to the company in exchange for an issue of shares in the company will be able to be held over for CGT purposes. The chargeable gains held over will be deducted from the acquisition cost (for CGT purposes) of the shares issued to the Name. Where a Name transfers their underwriting business to an SLP the normal rules for calculating any chargeable gains or allowable losses on the transfer of assets to a partnership will apply in relation to the transfer to the SLP of syndicate capacity and assets held as FAL.

The above provisions apply from 6 April 2004.

# Employees

### Employer-Supported Childcare

As announced in the Pre-Budget Report, from 6 April 2005 employees will be able to receive up to £50 per week of childcare, free of tax and National Insurance, where employers contract with an approved childcarer or provide vouchers to pay an approved carer.

To qualify, the benefit must be available to all employees and the childcare must be registered or approved.

### Foreign Earnings Deduction for Seafarers

The foreign earnings deduction is not available to workers on an 'offshore installation'. This term is currently defined by reference to health and safety legislation, but from 6 April 2004 will have a specific definition for tax purposes. This is announced as a tightening up of the rules.

### Company Car Tax

Where a car is made available for an employee's private use a taxable benefit will arise based on a percentage of the manufacturer's list price. The benefit percentage for 2003/04 is 15% of the list price where the $CO_2$ emissions are 155 g/km or less. The benefit percentage will increase by 1% for each 5 grams over and above the base level of 155 g/km. Diesels are subject to a 3% supplement unless they meet Euro IV emissions standards. The benefit percentage is capped at 35% for petrol and diesel cars.

In previous budgets the base level of emissions was reduced to 145 g/km for 2004/05 and 140 g/km for 2005/06. The 2004 Budget freezes the 2006/07 emissions base at 140 g/km.

The benefit percentage is also used to calculate any fuel benefit where fuel is provided for a private purpose. The benefit percentage was applied to a set figure of £14,400 in 2003/04. The set figure remains at £14,400 for 2004/05.

**Employer-Provided Vans**

Employees provided with a van that is available for private use, have a taxable benefit of £500 (or £350 for a van that is four or more years old at the end of the tax year). The benefit charge also includes any private fuel provided.

From 6 April 2005 a nil charge will apply to employees who have to take their van home and are not allowed other private use. Where private use is unrestricted the £500 or £350 rules will continue to apply.

From 6 April 2007 a van with unrestricted private use will have a flat benefit of £3,000 regardless of the age of the van. If an employer provides fuel for unrestricted private use an additional fuel charge of £500 will also apply.

**On-Call Emergency Vehicles**

Emergency service workers in the fire, police and ambulance services, are often required to take their vehicles home at night so they can respond quickly to emergencies. The current rules on employees' home-to-work travel mean that there is a tax and National Insurance contributions (NICs) charge when emergency service workers are required to take their emergency vehicles home when on call. The Budget measure removes the tax and NICs charges that arise in these circumstances and will be applicable from 6 April 2004 onwards.

**National Insurance Contributions**

Employers are currently able to ask employees receiving share options to agree to pay the employer's (secondary) Class 1 NICs liability arising on gains made from those options. Employees who agree to pay their employer's NICs liability under these limited circumstances benefit from a reduction in their taxable income equivalent to the amount of the employer's liability they agree to pay. Changes to tax legislation are necessary to provide the same income tax relief to employees who bear the employer's NICs liability due on post-acquisition earnings derived from restricted and convertible securities.

When securities acquired by way of a securities option are eventually disposed of, CGT may be due on their growth in value. Existing legislation ensures that the calculation of the CGT liability is unaffected by the income tax relief the employee benefited from when they paid their employer's NIC liability. This legislation needs to be amended to ensure that when employees pay employer's NICs on earnings from restricted and convertible securities, any CGT liability arising on disposal of those securities is not affected by the earlier income tax relief.

Minor changes will also be made to FA 2003 Sch 23, to ensure that the amount of corporation tax relief which the employer obtains when employees acquire employment-related shares is not affected if the employee pays the secondary NICs.

The relevant NICs Bill clauses will come into force at a time to be provided for by way of a Treasury Order following Royal Assent of the Act.

**Enterprise Management Incentives (EMI): Qualifying Subsidiaries Rule**

For EMI share options granted after 16 March 2004, the qualifying subsidiaries rule is changed in similar manner as for Venture Capital schemes above, so the company whose shares are the subject of the option is now allowed to have 51% subsidiaries.

# Corporation Tax

### New Minimum Rate on Certain Distributions

The government is concerned to prevent tax mitigation strategies that rely on incorporation and subsequent extraction of profits via dividends. For distributions on or after 1 April 2004 a minimum rate of corporation tax of 19% will apply where a company whose profits are below the threshold for the small companies' rate distributes profits to a non-company shareholder.

Special rules will apply where distributions exceed profits for the relevant accounting period.

### Requirement to Notify Start of Trading

The Finance Bill will contain a new requirement for companies to notify the Revenue of the commencement of trading. The three-month time limit will be backed by the penalty regime in TMA 1970 s 98.

### Management Expenses

With effect from 1 April 2004, it is proposed, as set out in the Pre-Budget Report, that relief for the expenses of managing investments ('management expenses') will become available to companies with investment business, whether or not they qualify as investment companies under the current legislation. The relief will also be extended to UK permanent establishments of non-resident companies and changes will be made to the way relief is given to life assurance companies for their expenses. The timing of the relief will change to align with accounting treatment and capital expenditure will be specifically excluded as a management expense deduction. It is proposed that the legislation will broadly follow the draft provisions published in December 2003.

### Transfer Pricing

With effect for profits arising on or after 1 April 2004, as set out in the Pre-Budget Report, it is proposed that the transfer pricing regime, which currently applies only to cross-border transactions, is extended to apply also to transactions within the UK. It is further proposed that the separate rules for thin capitalisation are abolished and subsumed with the transfer pricing regime. Small and medium-sized enterprises are to be exempt from the transfer pricing requirements except in relation to transactions with a related business in a territory with which the UK does not have a double tax treaty containing a suitable non-discrimination article and except where the Revenue requires (in exceptional circumstances) a medium-sized company to apply the rules. Dormant companies are also to be exempt as long as they remain dormant. There is to be a temporary relaxation of penalties until 31 March 2006, imposed for failing to keep evidence to demonstrate that transactions have been carried out at arm's length.

### Community Amateur Sports Clubs (CASCs)

Registered CASCs pay no tax on bank or building society interest and no corporation tax on chargeable gains reinvested in the club. Clubs with trading income or income from property below certain thresholds will also pay no corporation tax.

The Budget measures will double the corporation tax thresholds for registered CASCs. Consequently, CASCs will be exempt from corporation tax on profits derived from trading, if their trading income is less than £30,000 and on profits derived from property, if their gross property income is less than £20,000. CASCs that do not exceed these thresholds will not have to complete a tax return on an annual basis.

The above proposals will apply from 1 April 2004.

### Charities and Giving

The government is launching a Payroll Giving grant scheme. SMEs with fewer than 500 employees who set up new Payroll Giving schemes from April 2004 will be able to apply for a one-off grant payment to assist with the cost of establishing their scheme. The grant will be available for two years.

### Aligning Tax and Accounting

The law will be amended to ensure that companies choosing to adopt International Accounting Standards (IAS) will receive broadly equivalent tax treatment to those that continue to use UK Generally Accepted Accounting Practice (UK GAAP).

The revision will apply to accounting periods beginning on or after 1 January 2005. It will amend the legislation on loan relationships, derivative contracts, intangibles and R & D to accommodate accounting changes under both IAS and UK GAAP.

The detailed changes:

- Intangible fixed assets: where tax relief for amortisation of goodwill has been claimed, it will not be allowed again if goodwill is written up to original cost under IAS.
- R & D: claims will be allowed for revenue expenditure treated as added to the cost of an asset when it is incurred, rather than when amortised in the profit and loss account over later periods.
- Loan relationships: the concept of separate authorised accounting methods will be removed – except where a particular method must be followed for tax purposes. Certain assets with a derivative element will be divided into a loan relationships part and a derivative contracts part. Exchange gains and losses on certain loans can be matched.
- Derivative contracts: separate authorised accounting methods will no longer apply. Exchange gains and losses on certain currency contracts can be matched. Fair value gains and losses on certain hedging instruments can be deferred for tax purposes until gains and losses on the underlying item are recognised. There will be a coherent tax treatment for the derivative contract element of convertible and asset-linked loans and interest-linked gilts.
- Currency accounting: legislation will provide for cases where the presentation currency differs from the functional currency and will follow GAAP more closely.

### Derivatives

Some derivatives are currently excluded from the derivatives contracts regime established by FA 2002, because they derive their value from property or equities. The Chancellor announced that, following consultation, draft regulations will be made covering property derivatives, providing for gains or losses to be treated as chargeable gains unless the company is party to the contract for the purposes of its trade, in which case they would be treated as credits or debits as in the current derivative contracts regime. Gains and losses would be identified using the mechanics of the current derivative contracts legislation. The new rules would apply to contracts entered into on or after the date the regulations come into effect.

### Offshore Funds

The changes reform the tests to determine whether or not a fund qualifies for 'distributor status' and will apply from the first account period of an offshore fund ending on or after the date of Royal Assent. The aim of the changes is to bring more investments within the scope of being 'distributing' which will mean that a UK investor will have the same tax treatment as if they had invested in an equivalent UK fund.

The new rules reform the tests for distributor status in the following ways:

- The UK Equivalent Profits test, ie where at least 85% of their income as shown in their annual accounts must be distributed annually, will follow UK corporation tax rules more closely. Also, it will adopt the 'loan relationships' rules, used by all UK companies, in place of the 'accrued income scheme' rules applying for income tax.
- The investment restrictions will be abolished. Instead, if a fund crosses certain investment thresholds it must demonstrate that any underlying investments also satisfy the 'distributor' tests.
- Separate sub-funds and share classes of funds can now qualify on their own and will not be affected by non-qualifying sub-funds or share classes within the same fund.

Some consequential changes will also be made to the existing tax rules to ensure that an offshore income gain will arise where an investor switches between a non-distributing and a distributing share class of the same fund or sub-fund.

# Budget Summary

### Loan Relationships and Derivative Contracts

A number of changes are to be made to the corporation tax loan relationships and derivative contracts regimes, as follows.

- Measures are to be introduced for accounting periods beginning after 31 January 2004 to ensure the continued application of recommended accounting practices by open-ended investment companies when calculating the capital element of profits and losses on derivative contracts.
- The requirement that two persons with a major interest in a company have to make loans to the company before they are connected for certain purposes (such as restricting deductions for late-paid interest) is to be removed for accounting periods beginning after 16 March 2004.
- The rules restricting losses on derivative contracts with unallowable purposes are to be amended, to ensure that they work as originally intended, for accounting periods ending after 16 March 2004.
- Provisions are to be introduced to block an avoidance scheme which can apply where a company ceases to be UK-resident or where a non-resident company ceases (other than by disposal) to hold a loan relationship or derivative contract for the purposes of a UK permanent establishment. The provisions will apply to cessations on or after 17 March 2004.

### European Company Tax

The government intends to bring in the tax changes necessary to align tax law with the European Company Statute (ECS) in Finance Bill 2005.

The ECS, which applies directly as law in member states, comes into force on 8 October 2004. It permits the formation of a 'European Company' ('Societas Europaea' or 'SE') which will be subject to the tax law in the country in which it is resident.

The operative date of some of the necessary tax changes depends on the 'Mergers Directive' (MD) (90/434/EEC), which may have some impact on transactions which can be carried out to form SEs, or be entered into by them. The MD may not be finalised until 1 January 2005 or later. The government will consult on the changes required to allow for formation of SEs later in 2004.

# Capital Allowances

### Landlord's Energy Saving Allowance

A new allowance is to be introduced for landlords who incur capital expenditure on or after 6 April 2004 on installing loft or cavity wall insulation in a dwelling house which they let. The new rules will provide for a tax deduction for such expenditure up to a maximum of £1,500. The allowance will apply *for income tax purposes only* and the Treasury will have the power to add further types of qualifying expenditure by statutory instrument.

### First-Year Allowances

The rate of first-year allowances for expenditure incurred on most plant and machinery by small businesses is to be increased to 50% (from 40%) for a period of one year. For income tax purposes, the increased rate will apply to expenditure incurred on or after 6 April 2004, and for corporation tax purposes it will apply to expenditure incurred on or after 1 April 2004. The rate of first-year allowances for medium-sized businesses remains unchanged at 40%.

### Business Premises Renovation Allowance

As announced in the Pre-Budget Report, the government will introduce, subject to state aid approval, a Business Premises Renovation Allowance Scheme. The scheme will provide 100% capital allowances for the costs of renovating business properties in Enterprise Areas that have been vacant for at least a year. The scheme will be introduced in 2005.

# Inheritance Tax

### IHT Threshold

The inheritance tax threshold will be increased to £263,000 for new tax charges arising on or after 6 April 2004.

### Administration

Certain administrative changes will be made to simplify the reporting requirements of personal representatives (PRs) and where the IHT account is delivered late or includes negligent or fraudulent understatements.

It is intended to bring the IHT penalty rules in line with those for income tax and capital gains tax as follows:

- for a penalty to be charged (up to £3,000) for failure to submit an IHT account, or to notify the Inland Revenue if a disposition on death is varied, within 12 months of the account or notification being due;
- to change the current penalty provisions by removing the penalty charge where no additional IHT arises as a result of negligent or fraudulent material submitted to the Inland Revenue;
- to fix the penalty charge at £100 for the late delivery of an IHT account unless the tax involved is less than that amount or there is a reasonable excuse.

# Trusts

### The Rate Applicable to Trusts

With effect from 6 April 2004, the rate applicable to trusts is increased from 34% to 40%. This applies to:

- the income of discretionary and accumulation trusts other than dividend income;
- the capital gains of all trusts and estates of deceased persons in administration; and
- certain amounts received by all trusts (eg gains from offshore funds).

The separate trust tax rate of 25% applying to dividends and similar income received by trusts is increased to 32.5%.

ICTA 1988 s 677 (under which loans or other capital payments made by trustees to the settlor or their spouse are treated as the income of the settlor) will also be amended to ensure that the settlor is not given credit for more tax than the trustees have actually paid.

### Modernising the Tax System for Trusts

A package of measures is to be introduced to modernise the tax system for trusts. The measures are designed to simplify the regime for a large number of trusts (particularly those with relatively small amounts of income) and to bring the tax paid by trusts for the most vulnerable beneficiaries more in line with what it would have been had the beneficiaries held their assets directly. The provisions will apply from 6 April 2005 although certain measures designed to protect trusts for the vulnerable will be backdated to 6 April 2004. In detail:

- There will be a basic rate band applying to the first £500 of income for all trusts liable at the rate applicable to trusts. Trusts which receive all their income up to the basic rate band either net of tax or with an associated tax credit, will have no further tax to pay. Those which receive their income gross will have to pay tax at the basic or lower rate depending on the nature of the income. As a result, some 30,000 trusts will be taken out of the full self-assessment system, although to ensure that these trusts still comply with their obligations, returns will be issued to them every few years.

# Budget Summary

- There will be a new tax regime for trusts for the most vulnerable, allowing these trusts to be taxed on the basis of the vulnerable beneficiary's individual circumstances for both IT and CGT. Trustees will be able to use the individual beneficiary's personal allowances and starting and basic rate bands, rather than being taxed at the rate applicable to trusts. Exactly which trusts will be eligible for this new regime has yet to be decided but it should include trusts for the disabled and orphaned minor children.
- A set of common definitions and tests will be introduced for IT and CGT so that all trustees, especially lay trustees, can correctly determine their tax status and treatment.
- The Revenue will be working with the main representative bodies to develop better guidance on the correct treatment of trust management expenses under the law as it presently stands.

# Anti-Avoidance

### Disclosure Requirements

From a date yet to be announced, a new regime is to be introduced requiring promoters of certain tax-avoidance schemes and, in some cases, taxpayers using such schemes to disclose details of the scheme to the Inland Revenue. Penalties will apply for non-compliance. The new provisions will apply to schemes and arrangements if a main benefit is the obtaining of a tax advantage and certain other conditions are met. These further conditions will be designed to target schemes based on financial and employment-based products. The tax treatment of particular transactions remains unaffected.

Promoters of schemes within the new regime will have to provide a description of the scheme to the Revenue shortly after it is sold, including details of the types of transactions involved, the tax consequences and the statutory provisions relied upon. The Revenue will register each reported scheme and provide a reference number which the promoter will have to pass on to taxpayers using the scheme. Such taxpayers will then have to include the reference number on their tax returns. If a scheme within the new rules is purchased from a non-UK promoter or devised in-house, the taxpayer concerned will have to fulfil the disclosure requirements shortly after the scheme is purchased or first implemented.

### Avoidance Using Life Policies

Individuals will no longer be able to use life insurance policies to manufacture deficiency relief to avoid higher rate tax.

Deficiency relief applies when the final computation of gain when a policy ends, shows a deficit. As from 3 March 2004, the relief will only be available where the gains formed part of the same individual's income in an earlier year. This applies to all new life insurance policies (including capital redemption policies and life annuity contracts) and existing policies where benefits are increased, additional premiums paid or rights assigned.

### UK Equities

Where a dividend on equities is received on or after 6 November 2003, it is proposed that anti-avoidance measures announced on that day in respect of sale and repurchase (repo) or stock lending transactions will close a loophole whereby individuals are taxed on dividends at a rate of 32.5% but get relief for the corresponding manufactured payments against other income at 40%. The measures provide that a deduction for the manufactured dividend is only available to set against the dividend receipt and that no tax is treated as having been paid on the manufactured dividend received. Further measures proposed on 17 March 2004 and applying from that day extend the new provisions to trustees and provide that, where equities are disposed of, relief for the manufactured payment can be given only against the chargeable gain arising on the disposal.

### Companies in Partnership

A corporation tax charge will be made on a company in partnership where:

(a)     after 16 March 2004, the company realises all or part of its capital from the partnership over and above the amount it has contributed or invested; and

(b)     all or part of the increase in its capital is derived from profits, arising after 16 March 2004, that would have been taxable in the UK if the company's share of partnership profit were the same as its share of partnership capital.

The charge is on the amount realised or, if lower, the amount of profit calculated under (b) above. The measure is aimed at an avoidance device that seeks to save tax in certain circumstances by allocating partnership income and capital in different shares.

**Strips of Government Bonds**

For disposals of strips of government bonds after 14 January 2004 where a scheme or arrangement has been entered into to obtain a tax advantage, market value (computed solely by reference to publicly available pricing information) will be substituted for acquisition cost and disposal proceeds. Any capital loss accruing after 16 March 2004 from any such scheme or arrangement will be disregarded. Furthermore, a loss on an actual or deemed disposal (other than as part of a scheme or arrangement) of a strip acquired after 14 January 2004 will be disallowed to the extent that proceeds fall below acquisition cost.

**Double Benefit Leasing**

New rules are to be introduced to prevent the obtaining of a double tax benefit through the use of sale and leaseback, or lease and leaseback, transactions involving plant or machinery. The rules will apply to rental payments falling due under the leaseback arrangements on or after 17 March 2004, and will operate by restricting the tax deduction allowed to the lessee in respect of such payments. Lessors will effectively be taxed only on the finance charge element of the rental payments plus any part which recovers any capital expenditure on which capital allowances are available. There will be transitional provisions to prevent the avoidance of the new rules by terminating or assigning existing leases.

# Stamp Duty Land Tax

### Partnership Transactions

On the introduction of stamp duty land tax (SDLT) with effect from 1 December 2003, certain partnership transactions which involve an interest in land were excluded and remained within the scope of stamp duty. Such transactions are to be brought within the charge to SDLT with effect from the date of Royal Assent to the Finance Act. The transactions involved are where:

•     an interest in land is transferred into a partnership either by an existing partner or in exchange for an interest in the partnership;

•     arrangements are in place for the transfer by an existing partner of all or part of their partnership interest for money or money's worth to a person who is or becomes a partner, and the partnership property includes an interest in land;

•     arrangements are in place so that a person becomes a partner and an existing partner reduces his partnership share (or ceases to be a partner) and withdraws money or money's worth from the partnership, and the partnership property includes an interest in land; and

•     a partnership transfers an interest in land to a partner or former partner.

There are detailed rules determining the amount chargeable to SDLT in each case.

### Technical Clarifications

A number of changes are to be made to the stamp duty land tax (SDLT) regime. Except where indicated below, they apply with effect from 17 March 2004.

There will be anti-avoidance legislation to clarify the provisions for sub-sales where only part of the property is sub-sold. Legislation will also close loopholes that exploit the interaction between the provisions on sub-sales and those on group relief and sale-and-leaseback. The provisions relating to PFI projects will be amended to ensure that all such transactions are notifiable transactions. Changes to the legislation will ensure that the transitional provisions apply as intended to contracts entered into before the implementation date (1 December 2003) where there is a sub-sale post implementation.

There will also be clarification as to how the 'substantial performance' principle applies where the purchaser has a right to direct a conveyance to a third party.

Although in certain circumstances, works carried out on land after it has been purchased do not constitute chargeable consideration, an unintended SDLT charge may occur when a contract is later completed by conveyance. Changes will be made to prevent this.

An agreement for a lease which has been 'substantially performed' will be treated as a lease for most purposes. The Revenue intend this change to apply to all agreements for lease, regardless of when they were entered into. This also applies to missives of let in Scotland.

A variation that increases the term of a lease or the rent will be treated as the grant of a new lease. This applies to all leases irrespective of whether the original grant was within the scope of SDLT. All other variations will be disregarded.

Minor amendments will be made to the rules on surrenders and regrants of leases. Also, where a lease ends partway through the year, only the rent actually paid will be taken into account. Any rent for a period before the grant of a lease will be taxed as a premium.

There will be changes to ensure that shared ownership leases are treated in a similar way as under stamp duty.

There is no SDLT charge when property passes to a beneficiary under (or in satisfaction of an entitlement under) a will or intestacy. The legislation will be amended to put this beyond doubt. The amendment has effect for all transmissions of property since 1 December 2003.

The following provisions apply with effect from Royal Assent to the Finance Act 2004.

- The relief for 'chain-breaking', relocation and similar transactions will be extended to cases where the purchaser of a new house cannot move into it immediately, and stays on in his old house. The relief will be granted on condition that the purchaser does not stay in the old house for more than six months.
- The relief for sale-and-leaseback transactions will be extended to residential property. The relief will also be extended to include lease-and-leaseback transactions, and those where only part of the property is leased back.
- The acquisition of a freehold (or other major interest in land) where the consideration is less than £1,000 will cease to be a notifiable transaction. This also applies to the assignment of a short lease where there is no tax to pay, or no relief to be claimed. Such transactions may instead be self-certified. Furthermore, the acquisition of 'community interests in land' in Scotland will not be a notifiable transaction.
- Minor amendments to the legislation will ease the compliance burden in certain circumstances. There will also be comprehensive rules for claiming relief. Also, the legislation will be amended to provide that the Revenue will not charge two tax-geared penalties on the same amount of tax.

# Value Added Tax

### VAT Registration and Deregistration Limits

With effect from 1 April 2004, the VAT registration limit will be increased from £56,000 to £58,000. The deregistration limit will be increased from £54,000 to £56,000. The registration and deregistration limits for acquisitions from other EC countries are also increased from £56,000 to £58,000.

## VAT Car Fuel Scale Charges

The scale used to charge VAT on fuel used for private motoring in business cars will be increased from the start of the first VAT period beginning on or after 1 May 2004. The revised scale charges are as follows.

### Annual returns

| Cylinder capacity of vehicle | Scale charge diesel £ | VAT due per car £ | Scale charge petrol £ | VAT due per car £ |
|---|---|---|---|---|
| Up to 1,400 cc | 865 | 128.82 | 930 | 138.51 |
| 1,401 cc to 2,000 cc | 865 | 128.82 | 1,175 | 175.00 |
| 2,001 cc or more | 1,095 | 163.08 | 1,730 | 257.65 |

### Quarterly returns

| Cylinder capacity of vehicle | Scale charge diesel £ | VAT due per car £ | Scale charge petrol £ | VAT due per car £ |
|---|---|---|---|---|
| Up to 1,400 cc | 216 | 32.17 | 232 | 34.55 |
| 1,401 cc to 2,000 cc | 216 | 32.17 | 293 | 43.63 |
| 2,001 cc or more | 273 | 40.65 | 432 | 64.34 |

### Monthly returns

| Cylinder capacity of vehicle | Scale charge diesel £ | VAT due per car £ | Scale charge petrol £ | VAT due per car £ |
|---|---|---|---|---|
| Up to 1,400 cc | 72 | 10.72 | 77 | 11.46 |
| 1,401 cc to 2,000 cc | 72 | 10.72 | 97 | 14.44 |
| 2,001 cc or more | 91 | 13.55 | 144 | 21.44 |

## Annual Accounting Scheme for Small Businesses

With effect from 1 April 2004, the turnover limit for the annual accounting scheme (which allows businesses to make one VAT return each year, instead of four) is increased from £600,000 to £660,000. The limit at which existing users are required to withdraw from the scheme is increased from £750,000 to £825,000.

## Reduced Rate for Ground Source Heat Pumps

With effect from 1 June 2004, ground source heat pumps will be subject to the 5% reduced rate of VAT.

## Demonstrator Cars: Changes to Valuation Provisions

VAT on the purchase of demonstrator cars provided by motor dealers and manufacturers is excluded from the blocking order which generally prevents VAT recovery on the purchase of motor cars. Instead, VAT is due on the private use of such cars. Certain businesses have sought to minimise the VAT due on private usage by charging employees a nominal sum for the use of the car.

From a date to be announced, the Commissioners will be able to direct that VAT is to be accounted for on the open market value of demonstrator cars supplied to employees. This measure requires a derogation from European Community legislation; such a derogation has been applied for.

## Cash Accounting Scheme for Small Businesses

With effect from 1 April 2004, the turnover limit for the cash accounting scheme (which allows small businesses to account for VAT on the basis of the date of payment, rather than the date of the invoice) is increased from £600,000 to £660,000. The limit at which existing users are required to withdraw from the scheme is increased from £750,000 to £825,000.

# Budget Summary

In addition, businesses which leave the scheme (either voluntarily or because they have breached the £825,000 limit) will be able to account for any outstanding VAT due under the scheme on a cash basis for a further six months.

### Natural Gas and Electricity: Place of Supply

With effect from 1 January 2005, the place of supply of wholesale supplies of natural gas and electricity will be where the customer is established. VAT due on the supply will be accounted for by the reverse charge mechanism. Other supplies will take place where the natural gas or electricity is consumed.

Changes will also be made to the place of supply of services relating to the supply of natural gas and electricity.

The importation of natural gas and electricity from outside the EC will be relieved from VAT.

### Disclosure of the Use of Avoidance Schemes

With effect from a date to be announced following Royal Assent:

- businesses which make supplies of £600,000 or more will be required to disclose the use of any avoidance scheme which is included in a statutory list published by the Commissioners. Failure to disclose will give rise to a penalty of 15% of the tax avoided;
- businesses with supplies exceeding £10 million per year must disclose the use of schemes which have 'certain of the hallmarks of avoidance'. The disclosure must be made within 30 days of the due date for the first VAT return affected by the scheme. Disclosure is not required where the promoter of the scheme has registered it with the Commissioners. Failure to disclose will give rise to a penalty of £5000.

### Commercial Buildings: Anti-Avoidance

Anti-avoidance provisions come into effect from 18 March 2004, designed to block a complex avoidance scheme involving the need for co-operation of a third party developer and the establishment of a special purpose vehicle (SPV), either by the user of the building or the developer. The rules for transfer of going concerns (TOGC) and the option to tax will be amended.

There are two main variants of the avoidance scheme.

*TOGC with an opted property.* The amendments to close this scheme will:

- remove the de-supply of a TOGC in property in certain circumstances, so that the developer's supply of the freehold is taxable; and
- disapply the option to tax for the partly exempt user's SPV, causing the VAT on its purchase to 'stick' with it. This is done by requiring anyone making supplies under a lease (but who did not make the initial grant) to apply the option to tax disapplication test as though they had made a new grant.

*Sale of a company with taxed lease.* The measure will again close this variant by:

- where there is a TOGC, removing its de-supply so that the developer's supply of the freehold is taxable; and
- in all cases disapplying the developer's SPV's option to tax, causing the VAT on its purchase to 'stick' with it. The disapplication will be triggered where there is any consideration used to purchase shares or securities if this consideration originates from someone using the building for an exempt purpose.

### Revised Eligibility Rules for VAT Groups

With effect from 1 August 2004, the eligibility rules for VAT grouping are to be extended. Where a corporate body (jointly owned company or wholly owned subsidiary, including a limited liability partnership) run by a third party makes taxable supplies to a VAT group which is unable to fully recover VAT on such supplies, that body is not eligible to join the VAT group if:

- the majority of the economic benefits from the body go to a third party, or
- the body's accounts are not consolidated in the group accounts for the person controlling the VAT group.

The legislative changes will also make it clear that a corporate body cannot be in more than one VAT group at the same time.

# Taxes on Expenditure

### Alcohol Strategy: Duty Stamps for Spirits

To avoid loss of tax through spirits fraud, with effect from the date of Royal Assent to the Finance Act, retail containers of spirits will, subject to certain exceptions, be required to bear a duty stamp indicating that UK duty has been paid. Retail containers of wine or made-wine with an abv over 22% will also be subject to the same requirements.

### Alcohol Duty Rates

With effect from midnight on Sunday 21 March, the excise duty on beer and still wine will be increased by 3.01%, adding 1p to a pint of beer and 1p to a standard 175ml glass of wine. The excise duty on spirits, cider and sparkling wine is frozen.

### Alcohol Duties: Small Breweries' Relief

With effect from 1 June 2004, reduced rates of duty will be introduced for beer brewed by independent breweries which produce between 30,000 and 60,000 hectolitres per year. These reduced rates will taper from the reduced rate currently paid at a production level of 30,000 hectolitres per year to the full standard rate on production levels exceeding 60,000 hectolitres.

### Taxation of Pool Betting

Customs have announced that, for accounting periods ending on or after Royal Assent, all pool betting on dog racing or horse racing, where the promoter or the totalisator is based in the UK, will fall within the general betting duty provisions. All other pool betting, where the promoter or the totalisator is based in the UK, will fall within the pool betting duty provisions.

### Tobacco Products

With effect from 6pm on 17 March 2004, the rates of duty on tobacco products imported into, or manufactured in, the UK are increased in line with inflation. This will increase the price of a packet of cigarettes by approximately 9 pence.

### Hydrocarbon Oils

Excise duty rates on hydrocarbon oils will be amended with effect from 1 September 2004. A new rate of 48.52 pence per litre will be introduced for sulphur-free petrol and diesel. This is 0.5 pence per litre less than the duty rate for ultra-low sulphur petrol and diesel.

With effect from 1 January 2005, a new rate of 28.52 pence per litre will be introduced on bioethanol used (or set aside for use) as fuel in any engine, motor or other machinery, or as an additive or extender in any substance so used. This is 20 pence per litre below the prevailing rate for sulphur-free petrol.

With effect from Royal Assent, HODA 1979 will be amended to allow the mixing of duty-paid road fuels of different categories with each other without further duty charge.

The new requirements contained in Directive (EC) 2003/96 will be implemented into UK law by regulations to be made after Royal Assent. The changes are intended to facilitate intra-EU movement of dutiable products, but will not affect the scope or rate of duties in the UK.

# Budget Summary

### Gaming Duty: Changes to Duty Bands

With effect for accounting periods starting on or after 1 April 2004, the gross gaming yield (GGY) threshold for each duty band will be increased as follows.

| | |
|---|---|
| First £516,500 of GGY | 2.5% |
| Next £1,146,500 of GGY | 12.5% |
| Next £1,146,500 of GGY | 20% |
| Next £2,007,500 of GGY | 30% |
| Remainder | 40% |

### Amusement Machine Licence Duty: Changes in Duty Rates

With effect in relation to any licence applications received at Greenock Accounting Centre on or after 22 March 2004, the annual cost of licences is as follows:

| | |
|---|---|
| Category A | £250 (no change) |
| Category B | £665 |
| Category C | £715 |
| Category D | £1,415 |
| Category E | £1,915 |

# Environment and Resources

### Landfill Tax

With effect from 1 April 2004:

- the standard rate of landfill tax will be increased from £14 to £15 per tonne (the lower rate remaining unchanged at £2 per tonne); and
- the maximum credit that landfill site operators may claim against their annual landfill tax liability is increased from 6.5% to 6.8%.

With effect from 1 May 2004, the requirements for landfill site operators in Northern Ireland regarding preservation of records and evidence to support a claim for bad debt relief will be brought into line with the rest of Great Britain (ie six years unless a shorter period is agreed with C & E).

### Aggregates Levy: Northern Ireland Credit Scheme

Customs have announced an extension to the current five-year scheme providing relief from aggregates levy for aggregate used in processed products in Northern Ireland. Relief will be fixed at 80% of the full rate (currently £1.60 per tonne) until 31 March 2012.

### Climate Change Levy

Customs have announced that they intend to extend the eligibility criteria for climate change agreements to cover other energy-intensive sectors of industry not included within the existing agreements. All businesses in sectors that meet or exceed a 12% threshold of energy intensity will be eligible to enter a climate change agreement. The new criteria will not apply until the proposed measure has received 'state aid' clearance from the European Commission.

Customs have also announced that, with effect from Royal Assent, exemption from climate change levy under FA 2000 will be extended to include biodiesel and bioblend. The legislation will also be amended with effect from 1 January 2005 to ensure that leviable energy products used to create bioethanol continue to qualify for exemption when a new excise duty is introduced for that product.